The Lunar Nodes to Pars Fortuna: Journey and Goal

Rev. Alice Miller

ISBN: 978-0-86690-655-5

Cover Design: Jack Cipolla

Published by:
American Federation of Astrologers, Inc.
6535 S. Rural Road
Tempe, AZ 85283

www.astrologers.com

About the Author

Reverend Alice Miller has been a practicing professional astrologer since 1983. She worked at it part time until her second Saturn Return and retirement from the U.S. labor force, in 1996. From that time it has been her full time vocation and avocation.

For several years during the 1990s she taught astrology in Denver, Colorado, creating the texts for her classes. Upon urging from students, she published her first book in 1994, followed by two more in 1995, including this Node book. The American Federation of Astrologers published two of her books in1999 and 2000. Then in 2010, the 2000 publication of *Heralds of a New Age: Interceptions* was reissued in a much nicer edition, and soon followed by a second volume: *Intercepted Planets: Possibiliteies for a New Age*. These two are now available from major book stores and from www.amazon.com. In the interim, she continues to self-publish her other books.

Rev. Miller also writes for *Today's Astrologer*, the monthly journal of the American Federation of Astrologers, and occasionally does local speaking engagements. From her website, www.lifeprint-astrology.com, she does consultations and readings. On the site you can find a number of articles, inspirations, and sample readings, as well as a page for ordering her books. Questions and comments from readers are always welcome.

She publishes Spirit and Stars, a free newsletter; request a subscription by emiling astrominister1@yahoo.com.

Books by Rev. Alice Miller

These books are available from www.lifeprintastrology.com

Principles of Astrology: Planets, Signs & Houses

Dynamics of Astrology: Interpreting Aspects

Soul of Astrology: Inner Dimensions of the Modern Moon

The "Limits" of Astrology: Saturn for Today

Healing the Inner Child: The Astrology of Family Dysfunction

Retrograde Planets and Consciousness

Getting Birth Charts on Target

A Coven of Planets: A Pagan Astrology

A Kabbalistic Design of Planets

These books are available from the American Federation of Astrologers, www.astrologers.com, and from amazon.com:

Designs for a New Age: The Grand Cross, Mystic and Other Rectangles

Heralds of a New Age: Interceptions

Possibilities for a New Age: Intercepted Planets

Pagan Astrology for the Spirit and Soul

Foreword

Combining these two books—one about the Part of Fortune and one about the Lunar Nodes—into one book seems natural to me.

The *nodal axis* is the Nodes of the Moon. It is our thesis that these nodes refer to the type of consciousness rise that is inherent at birth and from which growth continues.

The Part of Fortune (Pars Fortuna) is actually a Lunar Ascendant. We have observed that the Part of Fortune only becomes active and available in later years, as consciousness rises. The natal Moon represents the foundation for our emotional body and it is entrained from our mother. As the years pass and we mature, we separate from what were essentially her feelings about life and about us. We then create a mature emotional structure described by Pars Fortuna, which we sometimes think of as the astral body.

The *fortunate* part of this is that, at advanced levels of awareness, Fortuna often brings us rewards which could be called rewards for spiritual growth.

Dedication

This book is gratefully dedicated to Miss Dee, who gave me valuable advice early in my career.

Thank you, Miss Dee!

Contents

Part I

The Nodes of the Moon: A New Approach

Introduction

The term *Nodes* refers to a pair of points that mark the intersection between the orbits of any two planets. Its meaning is usually limited to a crossing of the earth's orbit by that of another body. The most commonly noted nodal points on horoscopes are the North and the South Nodes of the Moon.

Nodes occur in pairs, showing the crossing from south latitude to north and from north latitude to south. The two nodes are placed directly opposite each other, in a specific sign polarity and house axis, and must be delineated from both perspectives. Lunar nodes travel in reverse order to the remainder of the chart in an 18.5-year cycle. It is this writer's belief that astrological elements that travel counter-clockwise refer to evolution and the consciousness expansion that accompanies it.

The lunar nodes mark the points where the moon's orbit, around the earth, crosses the earth's orbit around the sun. Each is an intersection, one northbound and one southbound. This writer teaches that the Sun/Spirit symbolizes the energy source from/by which terrestrial life is created. The Sun's sign describes the general intent of the incarnation and the type of energy required and supplied for it. Energy + Intent = Identity.

The Moon represents a transducer, transmitter or translator of that energy into form. She acts as channel (birth canal) and Soul, giving shape and direction to energy releases. Ultimately, she is a conductress of energy as it passes into and out of the solid/visible state. She acts as intermediary between Creative force/source and its creation, between Sun and Ascendant. Hers is the symbolic womb in which the spiritual seed forms an earth body. This body and its lifestyle are represented by the Ascendant and house structure. The body is the visible structure which permits the experience of form and consciousness.

The nodal axis then describes where being and intention come together and begin to expand awareness. The signs involved refer to your specific approach to evolution, and the houses show where that is most visible.

Summary of Currently Available Information

Research for this work took several forms. Existing published works offered some clues. Most writers feel that the North Node is a point of ingress and the South a point of egress, but no clear statement of what was entering and leaving or why it was happening was found. In the works studied, there was a general feeling that the nodal axis is related to the incarnational cycle with the South Node representing the past and the North Node the future.

Historically, I had associated this pattern with the work of Marc Robertson[1] on lunar cycles. I felt that his eight divisions were steps on the path from South Node to North Node. In general, clients resonated to this. The nodal axis became a marker of the direction of spiritual growth. Only recently did I realize that in a given incarnation the primary goal may not be growth.

Because the axis is involved in relational matters it is common to find links from the planets of one chart to the lunar nodes of another in close relationship. Experience shows that planetary persons[2] in our own chart or any significant point in the charts of those in close relationship to us influence the direction of our lives. Conjunctions and positive aspects to the North Node usually help us, or sometimes *shove* us, toward our internal goals. Because of them, emphasis, attention, or impetus is added to our personal motion. In some way they trigger emotion in us, moving us along.

Cross-chart aspects involving the South Nodes have a poor reputation and are usually taken to refer to unfinished karma. Practice suggests that South Node contacts from other charts are generally not pleasant. In more advanced charts, our karma is not a factor but the contact may show that we have some contribution to offer to the working out of the other person's karma. I suspect that it shows one who has been dependent on us in the past. This would create a familiarity and an attraction. The lesson to be learned may be that we must leave them to work out their own issues. When there are aspects between the nodes of one chart and planets or significant points of another,

---

[1] *Cosmopsychology I: The Engine of Destiny* by Marc Robertson, American Federaiton of Astrologers.
[2] Sun Father, Moon Mother, Mercury Sibling, Jupiter Teacher, Saturn Family Authority, Pluto family power or control.

all cross-aspects should be closely examined. Sometimes the contact represents nothing more than a need for completion.

Squares to the nodes, especially in our own chart, tend to pull attention away from the nodes in the beginning, but can act as an outlet[3] later in life. The one certainty is that when we have chart factors that aspect our lunar nodes, they will contribute to our awareness of the nodes in one way or another.

Beyond this, not much was discovered in existing literature. Still, almost every chart printed has the lunar modes marked. We seem to have a fascination for them, which suggests that we sense that the information they offer us is valuable. It seems appropriate to delve deeper.

---

[3]Similar to the way planets on the point of a Yod do.

Biblical Research

The North Node of the Moon has long been called The Dragon's Head and the South Node is referred to as the Dragon's Tail. As a longtime student of the Bible, I connected this with the allegories in the part of the Bible called The Revelation or The Apocalypse. I regard this book as a visionary distillation of the wisdom that has been channeled down through the ages. The specific part referred to is distinctly astrological in nature. Chapter 13, verses 1-2 state:

> And I stood upon the sand of the sea, and saw a beast rise up out of the sea, having seven heads and ten horns . . .[4]

> And the beast which I saw was like a leopard. His feet were the feet of a bear, and his mouth like the mouth of a lion. The dragon gave him his power, his throne and great authority.

Believing that most, perhaps all of the biblical prophecies are defined in astrological terms of the day. I interpret the above passage as follows:

1. Biblical scholars know that *beast* means living being.

   A. The beast rises out of the *sea* . . . of the unconscious, i.e., the twelfth house. It is the Ascendant, the sign that dominates the environmental factors of the chart and defines our human or *earth* image. It is significant to note that until recently the words *ascendant* and *horoscope* were used interchangeably. This suggests that in reality the visionary is using the word beast to refer to the entire house structure. My interpretation of this is "the ego structure."

   B. Most of the biblical beasts have characteristics of the bull/ox, the lion, and the eagle, with the face of a man. These symbols arise throughout the religions of the world. In astrology, they refer to the fixed/passive signs of relatively solid form—Taurus, Leo, Scorpio, and Aquarius.

   (1) Since the word priest has its roots in the idea of the lead oxen in a team, the symbol refers to our ability to become our own priest and to lead ourselves.

---

[4]At the time, there were seven known planets which ruled a zodiac that is currently ruled by ten planets.

(2) The lion is king; we have the inherent capacity to rule ourselves.

(3) The eagle gives the power to *fly*/rise in consciousness and become the Scorpio Mage (Magi) Magician.

(4) The Aquarian man is the man who is the conscious vessel of spiritual energies. The *ONE* as the *one*. This is the last level prior to full mastery in Pisces and the choice over whether to return to the seed form and be born again in Aries.

C. This beast is spotted . . . a leopard . . . and clumsy . . . bear feet. At first each ascendant is relatively unconscious, therefore "spotted" and "clumsy." The bear feet may be bare feet; i.e., unshod feet, like a child or prior to conditioning.

3. The dragon gives his power and his authority to the beast for a time. This suggests that early in our development, or prior to real awareness, the abilities shown by the nodes are absorbed into the ascendant. The spiritual energy is diverted to physical growth until the body has reached its appointed size. The dragon/nodes have a dual meaning—a psychological and a spiritual one—as does the house structure. Initially it feeds the ego; in the end it becomes a tool for the spirit[5].

4. Cross references to the word *dragon*[6] include *serpent and Satan.* (I do not believe in an objective Satan[7]. I consider him a thought form composed of errors in judgement, invented for the purpose of controlling the masses.) The dragon/serpent image is, then, a symbol for an idea or concept.[8]

A. *Dragon* is a winged serpent; i.e., a serpent who is capable of rising to a higher level.

B. *Dragon/Serpent* means "the seeing one," so we may be referring to psychic ability.

C. *A fiercely watchful female guardian or chaperone.*[9] The psychic abilities are generally regarded as feminine.

Note: In Webster's dictionary, just above the word *dragon*, is the word *dragoman*. One of its origins is an Aramaic[10] word that literally means "to speak" and is a Near Eastern word for an interpreter or professional guide. *Perhaps our DRAGON is really a DRAGOMAN, a guide in learning to "fly."*

---

[5]One might notice the different ways in which the psychic abilities are used.

[6]The Scofield Reference edition of the King James version of the Bible was used.

[7]The word Satan is a verb, meaning slippery. To the degree that a personification of evil exists in the general consciousness, Satan exists. Such a being has as much power as is given to it by those who believe in it. It has little or no power of its own and will disappear when no longer believed in.

[8]Remember that the visions recorded and the recording of them took place very early in the Piscean age, so the attitudes will reflect the Aryan Age idea that all spiritual knowledge was to be kept *occult*; i.e., hidden from the masses, in the hands of a few *chosen ones.* According to Judeo-Christian tradition, it was Jesus who started teaching this knowledge to the general population.

[9]Definitions are abstracted from *Webster's New World Dictionary*, third edition.

[10]The native language of Jesus, who is generally given credit for being the discarnate who channeled the information in Revelation to its writer.

Kundalini and the Nodes

Ancient spiritual texts speak of the Kundalini as an energy which lies coiled *like a snake* at the base of the spine. From this position it was expected to rise throughout a series of energy vortexes or chakras in the body. Originally there were thought to be only seven of these chakras and some writers correlated them to the seven original planets of the Piscean age. Gradually over time, those who study life in the context of these symbols/images have come to realize that there are ten or twelve major chakras and many minor ones.

If we realize that energy and consciousness are one, then the whole construct may seem more rational. Clearly human awareness begins at the level of personal survival, which is assigned to the *lowest* chakra centered near the organs of elimination. The next natural level is that of procreation, or survival of the species. After that come chakras that refer to other body processes, digestion, cardiovascular activity, etc. Following that, the throat chakra and the head. A little thought will show how these levels of awareness rise naturally as the species evolves from primitive through social to spiritual interests. The whole idea is probably not so complicated as the gurus made it. The level of chakra activity to be seen by sensitives probably provides a visual picture of their degree of awareness. It is not unlike our ability to read progress from a horoscope.

The spinal cord is the link between the various parts of the body and the brain. The image of it as an energy-conductor is a reasonable one. It seems likely that the astrological correspondent to the spinal chord is the axis of the lunar nodes. In the past, certain spiritual students were trained to *raise* this energy through the chakra system. Actually they were taught to visualize the energy rising and then pouring down over or through the body. This might be the fountain of life, referred to by Jesus of Nazareth. Many books have been written on the subject. Most are full of cautions against attempting this without a teacher.

With what we know of electricity, combined with a perception of the physical structure as an electromagnetic field, this seems appropriate. Quite reasonably, some people fear electricity. If you do not know how it works and how to use it, you should fear it. Lay beside that the fear attached to the Kundalini *Snake*. It does not take much thought to see how the Serpent came to be judged an evil force,[11] a Satanic being. When the only recognized form of electricity was lightning, we looked askance at it. Similarly, *turning on* or *turning up* the energy flow through our lives without giving it direction is likely to give you an *electric shock*, possibly even electrocute you.[12]

Before we increase the energy flow, it behooves us to learn the applications for it. If our awareness expands, our electrical field does change, seeming to *vibrate* at a higher level. People who are struck by lightning receive a jolt to the chakra system and often develop psychic abilities rather spontaneously.[13]

Imagine what would happen to such a one if she or he were convinced that such talents were evil. In validation, we have observed that people who expand their awareness beyond the limits of their learned beliefs will find that they have greater tolerance for ordinary house current. Electrical shocks will not be so painful as they were earlier in life.

If we increase light without a corresponding increase in love, the power generated in being can be quite destructive to self and/or others.[14] This is the explanation for *black* magicians and other users of destructive power. Any use of a life force for destruction of the quantity or quality of life is evil. Fortunately this is rare. Neither can it be absolute. Before it reaches the point of having no positive effects, it will *unplug* its user. Good always wins over evil and life always wins over death, for at the end of each incarnation, we are offered resurrection.

Parenthetical: This does not mean that rising consciousness has a smooth path. Because of the human tendency toward divided judgment, those with less awareness may look askance at your progress. If their Love function is weaker than their Light function, they may fear you. Fear is dangerous and triggers physical and/or psychic attacks. Do not accept their judgement. Use your consciousness to set boundaries of protection from destructive intent. This eliminates the problem of whether others change. Sometimes they do. Bible scholars will remember that St. Paul devoted several years to stamping out Christianity before being converted. Set barriers against actions, not persons.

For most of the world, there is a constant rise into the higher and higher realms of both light and love. This will happen naturally over time if not hindered by too-rigid beliefs in religious doctrines

---

[11]The word Satan is not a noun/name. It is a modifier and refers to the quality of being slick or slippery. There are reasons why a more simplistic consciousness would fear certain life forces, but with spiritual/soul maturity should come increased awareness/rising consciousness and with it the loss of negative judgments. Such loss frequently destroys traditional structures and certainly threatens those social structures which give one or a few individuals control over another or others. Jesus of Nazareth said, "Ye shall know the truth and the truth shall set you free."

[12]Think of the stories of a spontaneous rise in consciousness in those who have been struck by lightening or resurrected by the modern electro-shock method.

[13]Witness Dannion Brinkley; information available on the Web.

[14]If you are concerned, there is no problem. Those who use power negatively do not care. Examine natal Venus for validation; make note of its path of progression.

or other *moral laws*. So long as we use all our boundaries as simple goals to be achieved and then surpassed, we are in no danger of regressing into such negative uses of the light we receive. Being children of the Divine, our bias is to divinity. We are far better than most of us believe.

Objectively, this works through the creative power of the word. If we say that we are turning up the power or causing it to rise, it will, most certainly do that. If we truly do not understand it, the rise may be slow and sluggish, creating only minor changes in our lives. When we *believe that we know* but do not truly understand, we may create major eruptions in the flow of our lives. When we understand that we are learning to use new energies and practicing for something greater, when we are willing to begin small, we can gradually and safely learn to handle these new creative energies. A common experience of this type is that of creating a sum of money, but also creating a matching need for it. In time we learn to create more directly, but while we are learning the power itself will regulate our lives in a way that maintains a balance.

Subjectively, we are raising the focus of attention from the more basic life energies, to increasingly advanced ones. We begin as infants with a simple focus on survival. Without that one, nothing else has a chance. The second level is that point where creation and procreation can be directed to help in personal and species survival. From there our attention rises to higher and higher levels of human expression. We move from the purely physical concerns of *dense* form to the translucent awareness of Piscean Mastery. The difficulty has been that humanity has believed that life was a choice between being a *higher animal* and a *lesser god*. The reality is that *lesser gods formulate bodies based on the animalistic pattern for use in expanding awareness.* If the spiritual seeker attempts to destroy, throw away, or ignore the *lower* structures, she or he is attempting to live like a plant without roots or a house without a foundation. If you rise very high without roots or foundation, you will surely come crashing down in the first windstorm.[15]

---

[15]Compare to Matthew 7:24-27.

The Nodal Axis and Rising Consciousness

Every nodal axis points to the natural level of activation, at the time of birth. Only consciousness can focus outflow, so the South Node must be karmic to the extent that it shows a type of focused release that we already know. The North Node probably refers to the point at which the inflow is most conscious, a point that we recognize as energizing. When we feel a need for energy/attention, we look to the North Node and it nourishes us. If we are wise, if we have achieved balance, we will release that energy through the South Node area in ways that come easily and naturally to us and we will assume that energy balance will result. This requires an essential trust in the rationality of life's structures and the benevolence of their Source.

Earlier we said that the Moon symbolizes the channel through which energy passes from the Sun/Spirit to the Earth/Body. In this step the initial physical structure is created. If that structure is to remain in form indefinitely, the form must *be fed*. The vast majority of people must receive a certain amount of attention from conscious minds for our energy phase to remain within the perceptual range of the inhabitants of Earth. Only a few advanced souls have learned to ground, or draw sufficient energy from Earth to remain in visible form.[16]

Having become a physical form, we take on the physical feeling structure that becomes a communication system for the body. If the body does not receive adequate attention, it gets sick and/or painful, causing the child to cry. Any reaction to this crying will keep the body in form. Only being completely ignored will allow it to lose structure and visibility. Some infants cry a great deal to get the amount or type of attention they need to survive as what they are.

Others get attention by *acting cute* or by various other methods. As psychology, the North Node points to the methods that worked for the infant and will be natural in the adult. If the natural method has negative judgements on it, adults will not seek attention in ways appropriate to their needs. Sometimes adults have difficulty receiving at all, because they were so well-trained in giving to others during childhood. In these there is an assumption that the only way to get approval/

---

[16]Usually earth energy is best for physical healing.

energy is to give it first. Usually this does not work well until we get beyond the ego and its logical assumption that world population is divided into givers and takers.

At the social level, much co-dependant *feeding* goes on because there is a common belief that we need each other. If so, each must supply the other with energy; i.e., attention. It is as though being ignored makes us suffer. It is needful for *adults* to realize that—unless you live completely isolated from everyone—you will get enough energy to survive. This will be true even if you do not know that you can draw from earth, nature, sun, moon, and stars. The problem is that we have been conditioned to think that we have to have the exclusive love/attention of at least one other person, and we refuse to be happy without it.

We might describe the North Node of the Moon as a kind of funnel that directs this energy into a specific area of our psyche/sign and our life/house. At the South Node we give back to life the energy that has motivated and powered us. To the degree that we are conscious of both the inflow and the outflow, we use our ability to live consciously, directing the outflow back through the lunar channel. This allows it to be stepped up, even as it was originally stepped-down. Since any real understanding of the energy basis of life is new, the traditional attitude toward the nodal axis has been a bit superstitious and unclear.

I once asked my guides why so little is known about chart areas like Interceptions, Nodes, and Fortuna. He said that chart factors can only be understood as the general consciousness reaches particular levels. Today human consciousness is rising rapidly and more information on these is being released.

Nodes and the Ego Program

When we study methods of raising consciousness we learn that we are creators of our own reality. Whatever and however we *name* a thing determines how it must behave. For as long as we remain convinced that life works in the way taught during childhood by our parents, teachers, churches, etc., the solar/spirit/energy flow *must* create reality as we have believed it to be, and it will remain uncomfortable and often frustrating. In the earlier quotation from Revelation, it is suggested that this energy is in some way fed into the ego program.

It is for this reason that *natural* psychics who believe in devils and demons often see them. Their gift can only be channeled through whatever level of consciousness they have attained and their visions will take an expected form. Again we see some reason for referring to the serpent/dragon as a devil. This function will show you whatever you ask for. It is a little *slippery*.

Mundanely, the nodal axis often says something about money, especially at the house level, because money is generally regarded as the energy that runs modern society. It will also have some connection with relationship, simply because it is an axis that must have one end each in the personal and impersonal sectors of the chart. This can say something about which node is "mine"; i.e., which end I experience as self-generating, and which node seems to depend on others. Remember that such divisions are artificial constructs based on a misuse of the logical function. Reprogramming through visualizations, affirmations, or rituals can do much to change the learned attitudes which influence the function of nodes.

Consciousness and Tradition

It has been traditional to regard spiritual teachers as a group set apart, for whom the ordinary rules and laws do not apply. For the vast majority of Earthlings, the achievement of such a role was considered out of reach. Jesus of Nazareth was the first major teacher to say that enlightenment was for all and that even the most humble could learn its principles if they were translated into the common language. The foundation of magic and miracle is one of expanded consciousness as greater awareness of life principles. Necessarily, these were kept hidden/ esoteric until civilization reached a point where individuals no longer had to spend their lives focused entirely on personal and species survival. Even as individuals must reach physical adulthood before they can begin to expand personal awareness beyond the inherited base level, so also world population had to reach a certain *size* before world consciousness could rise. The possibility of that rise was predicted at the beginning of the Piscean Age. As it draws to a close, many individuals are feeling the necessity for raising awareness in the general population.

Ever more individuals are *being called*. Of those *called*, many have responded, coming to earth, not to grow and learn but to heal and teach. These often carry "the mark of the high calling of God[17]," the signature of the Starseed,[18] or the torch of the Lightbearer[19]. The astrological formation of this mark is discussed in our work on interceptions.

With or without that mark, if we are more focused on learning, growing, becoming, and/or perfecting ourselves, our *inner image*, will be based on the North Node. That will become our *Ascendant in consciousness* with the South Node acting as the Descendant. To whatever degree we think of ourselves as the dependant *little child* of god/goddess we will keep our focus on the intake at the North Node. The more fixated we are on the traditional religious beliefs the less aware we will be of any release at the South Node. An unconscious South Node releases only at the physical level, and then erratically. We can be *spiritually constipated*, with our giving limited to primitive levels with

---

[17]St. Paul.
[18]Brad Steiger.
[19]Barbara Marciniak and Barbara Hand Clow.

a short *self-life*. A free flowing South Node contributes to the rise of consciousness in the species. These lives are gifts to the eternality of LIFE.

Usually the entry into incarnational experience for the solar energy as shaped by the lunar channel and directed through the North Node should be entirely devoted to the physical for the first 18-year nodal cycle. It will usually be devoted to the social for at least one cycle after individuation is achieved. Historically, it is rare for any conscious attempt at using the Nodes to be made before the thirty-seventh year. (Today's New Kids may use them much earlier.)

It appears that the nodal axis may repeat several times over several incarnations, adding consciousness to its placement. Through it we have the opportunity to focus on one polarity at a time. To this degree the nodes point to a *spiritual* goal that might more accurately be called the goal of consciousness. This links to the idea that humanity is a *spark/molecule* of Deity, seeking to become more self-aware. Each nodal axis allows us to experience consciousness directly through its house and sign locations. Remember that consciousness is a result or side-effect of spirit living in form. It is the means by which spirit takes on and keeps a formal structure long enough to perceive, experience, and master the physical symbols of an abstract and invisible mental/spiritual construct.

The natal phase of the Moon adds information on the particular psychological type as defined by the current nodal development. The lunar phase seems to show where we are in the journey between the nodes at birth. If we regard the Ascendant as that point where world consciousness enters our life structure, we might equally say that the North Node is that point where Universal/God consciousness enters.

History has overlooked the fact that this is a set of points requiring us to release used energy. It must pass through our lives, to the next task. Energy does not get *used up*. It simply triggers activity. The modern image that describes its work is that of electrical current powering a unit, then passing on undiminished to power the next one. Even where there is some *loss*, there is a conversion of this minute energy quanta into a larger output of heat, light, motion. In the end we might say that the current passes though an electrical system to increase its effectiveness. Using this analogy, the North Node is where the energy current enters our personal structure and the South Node where it leaves and what it leaves in its wake. The South Node then becomes our gift to life.

Some who are intentionally holding to the past, rejecting any expansion of conscious awareness, will be very possessive of the South Node, refusing, inhibiting, and/or repressing any release there. These will literally *ground out* the life current. Some become *lightning rods* attracting great crises. Crisis may awaken them to greater levels of being. If the suppression continues it will produce bloating and/or constipation of the soul, with a corresponding poisoning of the emotions.

With an intense focus on avoiding or preventing release from the South Node, the North Node can be like a black hole that sucks in any free energy that comes near. These are the beings whom we sometimes call *energy parasites* or *vampires*. Not valuing life, wishing only to escape this world intact, but being afraid to let go and die, they live off the life energy generated by others. These beings are usually healthy, but it is common to find them pretending otherwise. Meanwhile those around them tend to have health difficulties that increase in severity over time. Notice the cases where someone cares for an invalid for years and then one day dies *suddenly*, leaving the *invalid* still alive. At this point, the *invalid* may make a remarkable recovery if there is no other victim handy. All too often a son or daughter gets the job of caring for a parent when a mate vacates the position. These can sometimes be predicted from aspects to nodes. This is primarily related to aspects within the native's own chart and secondarily of confirming inter-chart aspects.

Certain people who seek to win the approval they have not given to themselves, give to the point of damaging health and life. To do this for a long time will give the appearance and manifestation of depletion. This is behind much of the body and security trauma among good people. Here the South Node functions as the spiritual Ascendant because these people believe that the way to rise in value is to channel their life energy, their time and resources, into the life of another.

The natural functioning of the Nodes shows an emphasis on the North Node as the inner image when the Moon's phase is between new and full, because they are building a structure for a particular purpose. They are becoming the people who can fulfill their particular commitment to life.

For those persons born between the full Moon peak and the next new Moon, the emphasis will be on the South Node, as they contribute to raising the level of the general consciousness. In both cases the descending node must be allowed to function as it will. There must not be a closing or refusal of it, for we can only give what we have received, we can only receive what we are given. Any compulsiveness or control issues attached to either Node will retard spiritual growth and personal evolution.

Efficient functioning of life is achieved through recognizing the nodal axis as a direction or cycle of flow. We need to achieve a balance in which they *breathe*. This can be visualized as drawing in for release or as letting go to make space for receiving. Ultimately the outflow pulls in the inflow and/ or the inflow pushes out the outflow. If one is not judged more significant than the other, they will balance. Individuals then function as clear channels for energizing life on earth.

This is not to say that all natives with balanced Nodes will automatically be aware of themselves as channels. *This* will depend on the level of evolution that surrounds them. When there is balance and the balance is unconscious, the individual will probably be sexually fertile and/or exceptionally creative or productive within the social context. Earth channels commonly take themselves for granted, wondering what others are getting so excited about.

When there is little consciousness, this energy will just *escape* randomly and return to the state of *raw material*. While our consciousness is directed to physical concerns, and at first it must be, that energy will be directed into the Ascendant and house structure. It will simply power our learned (ego) beliefs about ourselves and about life. Always this energy will create something. It will create what we expect it to produce with results that we regard as negative, positive, or neutral. Those beings who are committed to certain *arrested* beliefs will be nearly as creative as those who are consciously and intentionally cooperating with the Source of life, but their creations will look entirely different.[20]

Always, a kind of *battle* between *good and evil* goes on. As humans evolve to higher levels of enlightenment, this battle between those who seek "life and greater life" and those wish to remain within the *moral laws* of an earlier age, gets intensified. It is sometimes referred to as Armageddon[21].

---

[20]If you want to *suffer for the Lord*, you can certainly create that. If you want poverty, so be it.

[21]Armageddon was the sight of a very intense battle which took place in Old Testament times. It came to be used as a generic term for intense struggles.

Using the Nodal Axis

Having established these parameters for assigning one node to function as an inner Ascendant and the other as its corollary Descendant, we continue to the next step. Any horizon used in a divinatory context tends to function like the two hands of an individual. Correlate any Ascendant to the dominant hand[22] and any Descendant to the other. We do not cut off our non-dominant hand but use it in support of the dominant one. Any point functioning as a Descendant is to be used for support and assistance to the more visible Ascendant point.

In any context, real growth requires a *breathing* process. Energy enters, is *digested*, and then the remainder is released. We may view this as a natural balance, correlating it to a world in which animals use oxygen and release carbon dioxide while plants use carbon dioxide and release oxygen. We may also correlate it to electrical systems in which the power is channeled through an appliance and passed on without having noticeably diminished. In either case we have a world that functions as a perpetual motion system. The only thing which can interfere with that is human consciousness.

Rulers over this world, we are direct descendants of the Creator. As our world was created through the power of the *WORD*, its function is helped or hindered by the power of our *word*. To the degree that our word agrees with Original Word, to the degree that we allow the One Mind to function/channel through our mind, our world is Heaven-on-Earth or Eden. To the degree that we do not, we live by the "sweat of our brow" in a world filled with pain and thistles.

The general consciousness has now risen to a level where it is critical to begin realizing how creative we are. Astrology is a wonderful tool for this. It allows us to learn how life works by presenting each of us with a personalized schematic (natal horoscope). We can develop our own abilities through the realization that we have them. In turn, many of us will pass on what we have learned. It is this action that flows as a South Node release.

At this level each of us is a teacher, a healer, or a direct creator; i.e., magician. The form taken by our teaching, healing, or creativity will be defined by the sign and house placement of the South Node.

---

[22]Reverse the natal chart, and renumber the houses, for left-handed persons before reading it.

Modes of Nodes

Cardinal or *Active* nodal axes are the catalysts of the chart. They individuate and connect; they are born and mature. These maintain the interest in the birth and continued existence of life, providing the impulse to move, to grow, to change.

Fixed or *Passive* nodal axes are the builders and creators who work with, building on, and generating from their cardinal beginnings. These maintain the structures of life which consciousness needs for development.

Mutable or *Breathing* signs originate, maintain, and expand consciousness/awareness. This is the information processing system of the developing god-man alliance.

All nodal axes must learn to breathe. The inflow and the outflow must connect in a way that makes them conscious and intentional. Life is not about simple becoming; it is about *becoming aware* of the inner potential. The *seed* must sprout and grow, produce a form, and reproduce in like manner. This occurs at the spiritual level of energy and intent. It occurs at the physical level of birth and rebirth. It occurs at the level of conscious awareness. The rising levels of consciousness trigger rising levels of vibration. These produce *higher intent* and more refined structures. And the cycle continues . . .

Cardinal/active polarities must choose to breathe. Fixed/passive polarities breathe naturally, from the *autonomic nervous system.* Both require us not to hinder the natural outflow/active and inflow/passive of life. Mutable/conscious polarities represent conscious, intentional breathing.

Planets Near or in Aspect with the North Node

These often represent persons (or types of persons) who in some way make us aware of the inflow at this Node. Because they encourage or discourage us, we seek with anticipation or out of desperation. In some cases negative aspects will refer to persons who attempt to prevent this reception. Even then the result is almost always positive because anything that affects a node causes it to attract your attention. The more attention you give it, the more it grows, matures, and/or activates. This will, as a side effect, cause your consciousness to rise further.

Planets Near or in Aspect with the South Node

These represent persons or types of persons who affect the outflow from your nodes in some way. They are often powerfully magnetic persons who live on your energy. Sometimes they coerce your energy into their projects. Occasionally they help in finding or provide the circumstances needed for an easy outflow. In some way they redirect your energy release.

South Node relationships often represent a Karmic demand.[23] The feeling that you must *fix* or *support* their lives is one that needs its meaning transformed. The key is that beyond a certain point in human development, to continue nurture is simply enabling the other to remain a spiritual child in an adult body. To do this inhibits the growth of both the parasite and the host.

If you have a tendency to attract people through your nodes, it would be well to clearly define what it is that you wish to attract and why. Be clear about the intent of your life and know that you can attract others who will support or share that intent. Affirmations, visualizations, or rituals can effectively activate, increase, or transform nodal activity.

To the aware, the North Node becomes the place where we allow SPIRIT to enter our lives. The South Node is the point where we release it to others and/or back to Source. The signs show what that energy *looks like*. The houses show where it is most easily found or released.

We do not always consciously know where South Node energy goes. It is only required that we let it go where and as it will, realizing that it is ours to use, but not to own or hold. In so doing, we become a positive force in the *spiritual ecology* of this earth.

Planets Square the Nodal Axis

Only the square aspect has the ability to affect both Nodes equally. Squares to the Nodes pull attention away. At best they prevent you from noticing where and how you give and receive attention. At worst they claim the attention of everyone else for their own issues. Here are some sample delineations:

Sun Square Nodes

Your very existence seems unimportant—to you or to anyone else on earth. If you survive, it can only be by miraculous means, or from a cosmic evolutionary level.

Self Realization is the only resolution, for once you know who/what you are, you can then become aware of how your consciousness works.

---

[23]When you have the *mark* spoken of above, *you* have no karma to fulfill, having done all that was needful in such matters. In such cases the karma is theirs. They refuse to release the relationship, demanding that their perceived needs be fulfilled. Your part in the matter is now, as it was in other times to force them to take the responsibility for themselves by abandoning them. World Consciousness, based on a perversion of altruism, often makes this difficult.

Moon Square Nodes

What you do or how you do it seems unimportant. A life without meaningful direction. Spaced out, maybe autistic.

Be aware that this *lack of direction* may be inherited from your mother, through your bond with her. Putting distance between you can help your discover your life intention.

Mercury Square Nodes

What you think or say seems unimportant. Nobody listens, not even you. Such a child might not learn to talk.

One way to resolve this is to learn another *language,* such as music, astrology, or computer coding.

Venus Square Nodes

Values, even the primary value—a body, seem unimportant. One taken for granted by self and others. Lack of self worth dulls consciousness. You may feel unworthy of education/consciousness expansion.

It will be critical to develop self-worth through the realization that "*God didn't make no junk.*" If you had no value you would not be here.

Mars Square Nodes

Ignored or unrecognized desires. Survival may seem unimportant because you can never have what you want.

This one can be easily *cured.* Although children are often taught that they cannot have desires, most are allowed needs. Transform desires to needs by realizing that anything you want is something spirit needs you to have.

Jupiter Square Nodes

Ignored or unrecognized growth. Feels like a *weed.* Like Topsy, this one *just growed*, without attention or care to how she or he developed. Unstructured, undisciplined.

All of this comes from a belief (not a truth). You can and will outgrow it, and discover what is true for you.

Saturn Square Nodes

Ignored, unrecognized, or assumed boundaries. Nobody set any because you were expected to know where they were. The need to establish some structure or formulae for life prohibits consciousness rise.

The simplest cure for this one is to learn grounding exercises. Once you can see your feet on the ground, you can reach for the stars.

Uranus Square Nodes

Disrupts focus by repolarizing attention. Attention was inconsistent and came from unexpected persons/places. You never know who is or is not watching. The uncertainty weakens energy flow. Late bloomers.

At some point you must realize that yours is a life of naturally constant change. Accepting that, begin to affirm that all change is for the better. This will convert the character of those changes to one that supports your life goals.

Neptune Square Nodes

Creates a tidal motion in the dynamics of life. Trust issues: you can't trust the attention you get. You do not trust yourself to pay attention as needed. This can make you hide your light under a bushel.

Exceptions might be Neptune and planets in Pisces or the Twelfth house—when they are conscious. Early in life, they would simply feel confused by the lack of attention, wondering what was *wrong* with them.

As with all Neptune aspects, this one is about teaching trust (faith). Realize that if you needed to see the path ahead, it would be visible. Simply *follow your feet* and trust the power that flows through your life.

Pluto Square Nodes

Controlled attention. Attention invested in something powerful, as a survival requirement. Abuse that interferes with development because it ignores your right to exist.

First, get yourself away from the person(s) represented by Pluto. Then use affirmations, visualizations and/or rituals to claim and own your personal power. It is your right and your heritage.

Nodes in the Signs

Cardinal nodes are active nodes. Always they are visibly *doing something*. The need for motion is conscious. When motion is seemingly blocked, life is painful and frustrating. It is important for these natives to understand that motion—whether in time or space—is relative. We are always at the center of our personal universe, and that is the only one that exists for us. Our personal space boundaries divide the me from the not me. Today divides past from future. When we have completed the cardinal journey, we are fully centered in the world, in our own evolutionary process, in the universe, in eternity. We can begin to realize that each of us is a *center of Deity*, not unlike the center of gravity in a planet. All else evolves around us. This will seem strange to many.

Modern holographs show us how this can be. Each of us is a holographic image of our maker, exactly as Deity stated its intent in the first chapter of Genesis. Breaking up a holographic image reveals that each piece contains the complete image. Astrology teaches us how to *break down* the components of any entity and discover that Original Being is always wholly present.

At whatever level or in whatever context, life is designed to move toward increasing awareness of its own nature. Periodically life returns to the being state to rest and regroup, but always it moves on. When it stops for an extended period it begins to die. Our earth provides us a nice example. We alternate day and night, sleep and activity. Whenever the night does not end, the earth will begin to die. It would be the same if there were no night; we would simply burn up or burn out. Life cycles similarly. When the cycle is destroyed, life is destroyed.

The simplest way in which to understand the active/cardinal polarities is to think of their placement in a natural chart. Aries-Libra is the plane of the horizon. Cancer-Capricorn is the meridian. Aries represents a birth of intent and correlates to a physical conception. The first three signs are like the three trimesters of pregnancy. At zero Cancer, life emerges from the dark of the womb into daylight. Its journey (or the current segment of the journey) begins. Cancer to Libra represents childhood and the growth process that culminates in taking our place in society at zero Libra. If we have been prepared and feel capable, this segment will reach apex and success at zero Capricorn. At this point, a particular incarnation or project reaches its peak and is the *farthest from the helpless-*

ness of birth that it will get. It has reached its limits, *within the context of the current definition of humanity.*

We leave the non-corporeal identification and enter a womb at Aries. We leave the womb and begin our incarnate journey at Cancer. We leave childhood and begin our social journey at Libra. We leave the social journey and begin our return to Source at Capricorn. It is important to realize that Capricorn is not an *ending*, but merely an apex. The form or structure may begin to deteriorate, *if we expect it to do so.* The intent is that, having reached the goal set for us by society, we can allow a new intent to be born and a new goal to be set. That goal will in some fashion be a return to Source. For those who have achieved little in the way of rising consciousness, it can be physical death or a regression into a *second childhood* of helplessness and dependency.

Aries-Libra

This is the first axis of identification. It is the recognition of me and not-me, each in the role of receiver at the North Node and giver at the South Node. This is the first sense of division in the totality. It is about the separation from the *pool* of *Deity/consciousness* which is the source of life at Aries, finding the apex of the cycle[24], and choosing whether to continue on the spiral path to greater realization. Separation is about sorting out the human form of life from the divine energy of life—the visible from the invisible, tangible from intangible. It is the foundation on which both structure and consciousness are built.

The Aries end of this axis is just awakening to consciousness. It begins to stir, gets our attention and we notice that this energy is me or mine. I am the one who receives it (North Node) or I am the one who gives it (South Node). Meanwhile the Libra end of the axis is at the full-Moon point, just beginning the opposite process. *I am not the only one* receiving (North Node) or releasing (South Node) the energy. Libra is the not-(merely)me; Libra is the Other/s. The Aries North Node receives energy from the totality and pours it into another or society.

Often the survival issue is present. Aries is personal survival energy. Libra is social survival energy. Partnership is a survival issue in such states. Aries North Node may avoid it as life-threatening. Libra North Node may feel compelled to be in a Libra relationship as a means of personal survival. The nodal axis is a type of ascendant and nearly always begins life split apart. In this axis, we sometimes see I-Thou as an adversarial relationship in which one loses identity and occasionally life.

Aries North Node must pay attention to self, and may not ignore self without risking the survival that is so important to him or her. Aries North Node is a giver and must become aware of receiving. She or he must learn to receive from the I AM or recognize that she or he does. Without this,

---

[24]Life takes a circular or cyclic path which is symbolized by the circuit of the zodiac. Libra is the point farthest from entry into incarnation, the apex. Its location can be lonely and frightening, we feel displaced, no longer identified with source and we must then choose to run back across the axis to Aries or to move onward through Scorpio and the remainder of the zodiac to complete the task and return to source at the end of Pisces.

she or he will drain self and resources in feeding another or others. Consciousness of the need for connection with Source begins here. Awareness of the relationship with Source is a necessity.

At the simplest level these nodes confine personal growth to marital issues. As they increase in complexity, they may show anything from an industrialist, providing jobs for others, to a pastor or priest. Literally, she or he becomes the administrator of the *Father's* estates, and/or an intermediary with Source. This makes balance and the awareness of receiving incredibly important. When it is not, such a placement can deteriorate into a host for a moral parasite.

Libra North Node receives energy/attention from a source like me but not me. The reception is seen as from an equal and the release further individuates or separates me from it. Sometimes this refers to being *pushed* to evolve by an adversarial relationship; i.e., by the need to escape. Such a placement belongs to one who is being pushed out of society, into leadership. Natives may change jobs or locations often, feeling the need to escape the *negative* pressure of those who surround him or her. Still they move, upward and onward, always trying to find peace, never realizing their leadership role. This can be a painful placement until the native realizes that his or her rightful place is one of leadership, and that she or he is not intended to *fit in*. (Leaders never do.)

This axis is the primitive, first level of life emerging out of pure existence. Aries says, "I am," "I exist." Libra is the first recognition of what is not-me. It says, "You are; you exist and you are separate from me." This functions on several levels.

On the Aries side, it is the infant realizing that it is no longer part of the body of its mother. It is the individual, realizing that it exists independent of society. It is humanity recognizing separation from its god-source.

On the Libra side, it can get caught in judgment and spend its energy trying to choose between being in body or out, between single or married life, between living alone or entering society.

This axis is about seeing both my similarities (Libra) to others and my differences (Aries) from them. Aries is the birth of separation and Libra is the birth of connection. At Aries we give up the security of heaven to begin a journey into consciousness. We leave Eden. At Libra we reach the full extent of separation that is safe or possible. We are individualized enough for our task and we begin the return journey by connecting with others who, although separate from us, are of like intent. Having left our initial home, we find a mate and begin to build a new one. Having released, or at least moved away from, our birth family, we establish a family of our own, a new generation.

At the metaphysical level, we establish a family in consciousness, beginning the formation of groups at the level of individual relationship. At a *higher* level we see that we are both separate and connected because we have the capacity to see ourselves both ways. At the highest level, the peak realization of these nodes, we understand that we are both human and divine, depending on how we are focusing at any given point. It is here that we learn to live *in the world, but not of it.*

The natural and easy direction for these nodes is with Aries on the North and Libra on the south, because the Libra point feels *older*, and farther from its point of origin. We are accustomed to perceiving spirit as something that we receive. Our belief systems have not generally included the idea of giving or releasing spirit from our form. We can think of receiving from Deity and giving to Humanity. To receive from Humanity and give to Deity seems a bit arrogant to many people. As consciousness expands, we begin to see life as energy systems. We may discover that the energy/spirit received is not *used up*, that it passes through our being, energizing and catalyzing it, and then moves on to continue the process. When, by our beliefs, we hinder that release, we set up resistance that slows the process and makes it less efficient. The most obvious results are poor health and restrictions in the economic flow.

Aries-Libra is the axis that demands sharing and balance. It suggests that the right side must have equal weight with the left, the top with the bottom, the inner with the outer. When applied to nodes, it requires that the outgoing energy must be of similar volume and quality with the incoming energy. We must not ask for more than we are willing to give and share if we do not want our energy systems to clog up. We must accept as much as we give, else we become depleted, suffering from spiritual anemia.

Ultimately this axis refers to the basic metaphysics of life. Each human *I am* emerges from the great *I AM*, evolves its seed of consciousness through the twelve-fold cycle of human evolution and returns to Source, bringing its gifts. Those gifts had their origin, in seed form, in the Source from which each individual spirit sprang. Without the journey in physical form, consciousness does not develop and grow. When there is no change, no motion, no growth, life is arrested and soon begins to die. Each of us is derived from the Whole and returns to the Whole. It is the process between that is the basis for the eternality of life.

The Aries-Libra lunar nodes forever reiterate a statement from Exodus 10[25], rephrased here:

> I am what you are. You are what I am. You are one side of the equation. I am the other.
> We are not separate except in your perception. Together we make up the whole.

On the invisible side of life is beingness. Beingness is perfect, whole and complete. It has no impulse to move, grow, change. It has a strong tendency to remain in existence, but does not LIVE. On the visible side of life is consciousness. Consciousness wants to live, to survive. Consciousness has the capacity to see itself, and especially to see itself as imperfect, divided, and incomplete. It is this capacity that drives it to seek more and more awareness of self and of its world. Through the process of human evolution we become aware of our godhood. We are the only means that the god-being has of knowing Itself, of knowing anything. In the end, God holds the key to creation but man holds the key to evolution. Without both, life is impossible. The two are and ever must be in partnership.

At its best, the Aries North Node gives God-realization to Man so that we may understand that we can depend on Spirit for our needs and desires. The Libra North Node gives Human-realization to God so that we may realize that Spirit depends on us and that we are not forever children to be

---

[25]Second book of the Bible. Original translation is "I AM THAT I AM."

sheltered and protected but heirs intended to become managers and co-creators of the very Kingdom of heaven. Through the revolving process the whole learns to know itself as the parts and each part learns to know itself as the whole. Which end is the entry point and which the release point is simply a matter of whether we regard ourselves as a part of the whole, or a whole composed of many parts. It is only perspective.

The Aries North Node is focused on individualization, on identifying as a part. The Libra North Node is focused on socialization, on identifying with society. The Libra South Node is a giver, the Aries South Node is a gift. These must relate and share, balancing the intake with the outflow. The two nodes must form a partnership. This is true of both directions of flow. Aries North Node signifies God becoming Man. Libra North Node signifies Man becoming God. These are the sum and boundaries of LIFE.

Cancer-Capricorn

The Aries-Libra axis is, essentially, about space. It is about defining and determining the amount of space between us and any other. In the same way, the Cancer-Capricorn axis is about time. It is the part of the Being Structure that helps us to center and be here now. Whatever the identification and relationship defined by Aries-Libra, it must be in the current time-space if it is going to affect or be affected by the current incarnation. Whenever we allow our sense of self to be stuck in the past, whenever we defer our living until some future time or circumstance arrives, we do not fully live. Life requires movement, growth, and change. It can tolerate stasis for short rest, review, and consolidation periods but cannot remain still for long. It will move in some direction; forbidden to progress/evolve, it will begin to regress/devolve. If we keep our focus in yesterday too long, consciousness begins to recede to earlier levels. If we defer our living until tomorrow, our progress stays somewhere ahead of us. The only place where we can be, become, change, grow, learn or teach is today. The Cancer-Capricorn nodes teach us to center and integrate childlike innocence with adult maturity. Its realization is that, without interference, all children contain the seeds of adulthood and that true adulthood must rest on a foundation of childhood. This is the conceptual model on which the theory and practice of reincarnation are built. Full realization of this axis will free us from the karmic mandate and give us choice in the matter.

Historically, Cancer has referred to the physical origins; i.e., the fetal state and the womb, birth and infancy. It is the fully dependant state. In the same vein, Capricorn has referred to the fully mature and adult state, to independence and responsibility, and to success on social terms.[26] For those whose roots include the more limited versions of *Christian* Theology, Cancer might represent hell and Capricorn heaven, with earth and the individual caught somewhere between. This doctrine has produced a segment of the population who believes that earth is a poor, difficult, painful

---

[26]Cancer's connection with mother is that, during gestation and early infancy she is perceived as an extension of ourself. Capricorn's connection with father is that he is our symbol for going out into society and, in traditional family structures, he sets the limits and administers discipline.

place to be and that being here is a punishment or mark of failure. In these same individuals there is also fear—fear that if they leave earth they may not have enough *positive points*; who can know how many are required? This can result in being relegated to the *local dump*, otherwise known as hell. This group, with their burden of fear, is probably the most destructive force on the planet at this time, for a rising consciousness is also a relatively undefended one. Those who seek to lift the general consciousness are often victimized by the fears of people whom they love and their energy is depleted. It is this struggle that has been called Armageddon.

This nodal axis, as a time link in the Being Structure, provides continuity and points to a cycling into and out of physical form and/or earth experience. It encourages us to realize where we are located in time and space, and to understand that wherever or whenever we are, all the activity must occur in the here and now. Whenever we allow our sense of self to be stuck in the past, whenever we defer our living until some future time or circumstance arrives, we do not fully live. If we keep our focus in yesterday too long, we will begin to regress to earlier levels of consciousness. If we defer our living until tomorrow, we defer it permanently; tomorrow never really comes. The only place where we can be, become, change, grow, learn, or teach is today.

Historically, the *natural* flow has been considered to be from Cancer/birth/infancy to Capricorn/middle age/adulthood. Since this parallels physical development, unless there is interference, we expect it and usually do not *stand in our own light*. We begin helpless and dependant; we pray for the simplest basics of life and our relationship to Deity is very much as child to parent. Gradually our prayers are for assistance as we learn, practice, and master the many facets of life; we are *growing up*. The natural outcome of the Capricorn South Node is competency, independence, and maturity.

Cancer North Node is newly born into a cycle and growing fast. It is not very conscious yet, and is centered on its own growth process. Its energy release will be directed into future goals quite naturally. She or he will not think much about it. It will be the essential growth process that attracts energy/attention from more mature beings and assists in the growth in consciousness. This can apply in either social or spiritual growth areas. The point is the growth in awareness that widens horizons and results in greater maturity. These beings are very busy *growing up* in one sense or another. They are preparing for responsibility but not yet there. With independence and responsibility as the South Node goal, energy may be *stored* for later release.

The growth referred to is the expansion of awareness, to see and experience more of life. How that growth looks is not so important as that it occurs. The placement can show a social climber or growth energy poured into career. It can also be a spiritual seeker. The only mandate is that the growth has a goal, so that when that goal is reached the energy can be redirected into a new birth of a new phase.

With full consciousness, Capricorn will simply refer to beginning a new phase in living, not essentially different from our entrance into society at Libra. With *arrested* consciousness, it will be the point at which physical incarnation ends and the wheel of karma turns, to dump us into yet another attempt at perfection. With *fully logical* consciousness, reaching the peak of progression means the beginning of regression. At certain levels this produces Alzheimers and other dementias, or the lingering death of a deteriorating body.

New phases of Capricorn can take a variety of forms. This can be the time when we achieve the independence of spirit that allows us full self expression without the restrictions imposed by social rules and traditions. It can be the time when, having fulfilled our *duties* to others, we invest our energy and attention in fulfilling lifelong dreams of many shapes and forms. Occasionally it offers us a new career. Some use retirement to *catch up on* lost playtime. Whatever form these new phases take, they represent our access to the unlimited wisdom of Sagittarius and the unlimited knowledge of Aquarius. Having demonstrated our current *limits of competency,* we turn away from them to return to earlier states or to move beyond them.

Beyond zero Capricorn, we move out of the arena of the general consciousness—one way or the other.

Capricorn North Node inflow can be restricted by a cold, cramped, personality *if we have not understood the extent of growth and evolution available to humanity.* Because we have not seen much beyond the parental god/goddess, we have not set goals much beyond the capacity to parent and provide for our own children. A successful career and a family grown to adulthood is as far as the general consciousness normally sees. Traditionally, the Capricorn North Node has regarded any further birth or growth at Cancer South Node as belonging to another incarnation. Considering themselves at an end of the growth cycle, many reject or limit the energy received. Life slows, becomes more solid and rigid. The energy flow sometimes reverts to a trickle and diseases of the skeleton can set in as the paralysis of spirit reflects in the body. This might be associated with the appearance of body rigidity early in life.

Capricorn North Node in some way denies childhood by *feeding* only adult energy. This should tell us that we are dealing with a mature being. Often it reverses the course of an individual incarnation so that the early years are difficult. Children can be expected to carry so much responsibility that taking on more and more during life becomes overwhelming. They feel defeated or tired, and long for death and an ending to pain. This makes them old before their time or leaves them feeling disconnected from their own future. In severe cases, addictions may develop, allowing their continued survival.

In most traditional belief systems, to be born old leaves nowhere to go. If too much responsibility is given to the child, the only way the Capricorn independence can be asserted may be to refuse all responsibility. Adults with this axis sometimes revert to childish behavior learned from the physically older persons who modeled it as adult behavior, producing *old* children and childish adults. These natives do more harm to themselves than to anyone else. In refusing growth, they refuse the rights and responsibilities that are their heritage as advanced beings and short-circuit their own evolutionary process. They begin to regress and to lose abilities that they had earlier in life. This may be ascribed to the physical deterioration of advanced age. The truth is that both mental and physical deterioration are results of giving away the energy resources of their bodies at the South

Node without allowing themselves to be replenished at the North Node. When reincarnation is rejected, the Cancer South Node can only produce a pseudo-childhood, either senile dementia or the more comfortable variety in which retirement offers the opportunity to do the playing which was denied in childhood. Arrested development is a likely cause of *repeat* lifetimes, where we seem to be going over old territory.

One way to give a traditional appearance to this is to become a parent. These may devote much energy to children (in form or consciousness), feeling that their only hope of immortality is to parent the future. Often this takes the form of frustrating attempts to discipline the new growth around them. These can be the most dogmatic leaders around. They will attract followers who are afraid to take responsibility for themselves and frustrate those whose intent is growth. These are authoritarian *father-types* who sometimes force the growth of their own children (as in Libra North Nodes) who feel the need to rebel.

Enlightened Capricorn North Nodes willingly receive a naturally self-limited flow of energy allowing it to complete any unfinished tasks from prior incarnations. They know that the next step is a rebirth and understand that in the completion of one task lie the seeds of the next cycle. If these nodes are very active, the incarnation may contain a series of rebirth experiences. Occasionally, they are found in persons who experience physical resurrection, who die and are revived–sometimes repeatedly.[27]

As the outer planets transited Capricorn in the 1990s, we were offered an opportunity to redefine, change, and release our limits. In time, with Pluto transits, we gain power over them and have more conscious control of the process. The opportunity offered is that of realizing that the Capricorn Node is not so much *old*—we have too many negative associations with that—as it is *mature*. It has an inherent sense of its own limits. It was born responsible. Since, to get to this point, it must once (earlier incarnations) have been a child, it is offered the opportunity to synthesize the innocence of childhood with the responsiveness of a mature adult. This synthesis is one that leads to mastery and new being levels. It allows us to know how much we can and should be doing for ourselves and when to ask for and accept help from a *higher or greater* power.

The final reality is that the Capricorn North Node belongs to one who is an adult in the present reality but a child in another closely-related one. With a shift in perspective, it is possible to have anything if we do our part without taking on more responsibility than we can handle. Over the course of a lifetime, the adult inflow will create rebirth and transformation at the Cancer South Node.

Cancer at the North is birth; Cancer at the South is rebirth. It is that simple. It presents a picture of step-by-step advancement on our path to full realization and integration with Source.

The axis is about making the process of human development conscious at the levels of body, soul, consciousness, and spirit. It teaches us that the human developmental process is a symbol for the

---

[27]Watch for an intercepted Fortuna, which is common to natives who have undergone CPR—or been struck by lightning!

overall process of evolving the *Child of God* from a *little child to a mature, adult son/daughter of Deity*. In time we realize that this is a revolving process that leads to higher and higher states of evolution and levels of vibration. Through this experience, we can sense a multilevel structure of life in which the adults of one level are the children of the next. It can also bring the awareness that the individual identity contains a family of aspects/facets that are accessible to us as angels and guides.

Sometimes with *younger* moons—new, crescent, first quarter—little apparent progress is made under a Cancer North Node. Still, it behooves us to realize that children grow and develop at different rates whether the particular childhood is physical, mental, emotional, or spiritual. Let there be no judgement on this. Life is eternal; we have all the time we need.[28]

Fixed Nodes

Fixed Nodes are passive or receptive nodes. The only thing *fixed* about them is that form, once established, must be fed to retain its integrity. They represent magnetic poles that formulate, activate, control, and adapt the physical structures of beings.

Whenever we incarnate on earth, visible physical structure becomes a given. Perceptual functions—the five senses—are necessary to begin the expansion of consciousness/awareness. The senses are functions of form. The development of senses makes awareness of existing form possible. It matters not. The reality is that this construct—despite the order of cause and effect—is the necessity for any real expansion of self-awareness, social and/or spiritual consciousness. When we list the modes in the order of cardinal, fixed, and mutable, we imply intent, formulation, and realization. Ultimately that is what the various modes refer to.

Passive nodes are directed toward the construction, activation, empowerment, or evolution of physical/visible forms. Once established, these forms, whether physical, social, personal, or societal, tend to be self-maintaining. They have the capacity to attract whatever energy flows, forms, or types are required to keep them in the realm of the visible. We say that living beings have a *survival instinct*. That is a spiritual capacity which is dedicated to physical survival at need.

Physical structures, once established, require total withdrawal of attention to fully release the energy they contain. Even a *dead* body takes some time to disintegrate after the spirit has gone. In cases where the attention of this being remains on or near earth from some sense of incompleteness or is held there by excessive remembering, the soul form or astral body keeps its earth connection and the form does not fully dissolve until all parties concerned move their attention elsewhere.

When the nodal axis is passive, the energy flows are being dictated by the needs of formal structure. For these natives the spiritual life and the intellect must be focused on the establishment, maintenance, control, or evolution of the visible/tangible aspects of life. It is about supplying the needs of the body, the society, and/or world that we live in.

---

[28]This can be particularly frustrating in the intercepted charts of the new Aquarians. The missions of these are *always* set to begin at some time later in life. Some may not be intended to emerge until a later incarnation.

Taurus-Scorpio

The Taurus-Scorpio Nodal Axis is that of form and reform. The Taurus North Node attracts or magnetizes the substance required to feed and supply the needs of physical structures—the body, the family, the local and extended social structures, and/or the world. Mundanely, Taurus symbolizes food and money or other possessions that can be easily converted to cash and then to whatever is needed for the growth and maintenance of physical life. Symbolically, it is substance that is ingested, digested, and excreted at the Scorpio South Node.

The Taurus end of this axis is new construction. It is about attracting substantial values, a body, and a supply of those things that maintain the body by attracting needed substance. Its principle is *like attracts like* and its realization is that self-worth is the requirement for expansion of influence, power, and knowledge. These are the means by which physical life retains, expands, and changes form.

Taurus is about loving the form that manifests from loving attention to the living energy or light of life. Scientifically, it is about finding and magnetizing matter/photons in the light stream of life. It integrates components into structures of value. It includes such diverse activities as cooking, making concrete, and turning forests into cities. The Scorpio outcome of such activity is the investment of individual ingredients, into finished products such as a dish or the structures that house, shelter, and protect humans.

Traditionally, we have judged Scorpio and its releases to be smelly, messy, and unpleasant. Some have mourned the loss of the natural elements that have been invested in improving conditions for society, not realizing that spirit always provides for its own. Because of this we have harshly judged Scorpio outcomes. Seldom has the very real value of so-called waste products been examined. At the most basic levels we find that fecal matter is excellent fertilizer for the plants that feed the world. This is only the beginning.

Food eaten in Taurus is converted to several uses. Part is used for the maintenance of the existing structure.[29] Form maintains form. Part is converted to *electrical* energy, feeding its mobility, with the secondary result of contributing to the health and welfare of self and others. Some small part is dedicated to reproduction. The remainder is excreted in a more concentrated form than it entered. Examination would reveal that the *livingness* in this excretion is nearly equal to that in its original form—even after it has performed the functions for which it was ingested. How dare we condemn that?

At another level, money—also not loved so well as it should be—is the *food* that feeds civilization. We have corrupted the original statement, "The love of money is the root of all evil." It is common to omit the first two words, leaving out the love.

The original statement refers to stockpiling beyond an amount that can be used and reminds us that stasis results in death. Quantities of money beyond needed operating capital must be invested

---

[29]The amount needed for this purpose tends to decrease as consciousness rises.

where they will grow. More than that, it needs to be valued—not as a *decoration* for our lives—not as proof of our personal worth—but as energy to be used in the production of beauty and/or comfort in life.

In summary, the lesson of these nodes is that form never truly dies; it is merely converted to energy or to another form. The chemical world is a symbol that shows us that we may exist in solidly visible, liquid translucent, or gaseous invisible states; but our essential integrity or *form* is eternal. It is the conversion of matter from one form to another which provides the vehicles necessary for the growth in consciousness that *is* life. A significant portion of our experience on earth is dedicated to the realization that life is eternal and that we are the eternal factors in it.

Another, symbolic, version of this is physical intercourse. Here the body connection and its accompanying activity merges two auras for a time. Two bodies/Taurus come together and fuse/Scorpio resulting in the generation and release of power. Consciously directed energy release results in creation. Procreation may be either conscious or unconscious. Currently, most procreation hinges on a simple belief or fear that sex leads to it.

When neither occurs, when sexual activity occurs at the purely instinctive level, from a belief that it is a *natural* drive, the release becomes free-floating energy, subject to being appropriated by any passing entity—unless it has been directed to a chosen task or creation.

It is for this reason that sexual activity has received so much attention in the religions of the world. In terms of life energy, one night stands equal leaving money lying around. You lose something you can't afford.

Whenever anything merges or fuses, energy is generated and then released in a fashion pictured by dynamite and by modern bombs. When uncontrolled it can function as free-floating anxiety, anger, compulsions, etc. When controlled and directed by an aware consciousness it becomes productive. It can be used to reform or transform, create or destroy, formal structures and/or to motivate or regenerate life.[30]

The Scorpio North Node represents an intake of power which must be released from form at the Taurus South. Sometimes birth feels like death and it is quite traumatic because when a discarnate spirit incarnates it is a kind of death. The underlying goal of any spirit with these nodes is learning about overcoming the fears attached to the greatest changes which life ever makes, the change from spirit to form and from form to spirit. In the scientific world this is called changing from energy to matter and from matter to energy. In the end this is no more and no less significant that the changing of any element from a gaseous, to a liquid, to a solid state.

Many have gone through dramatic personal transformation. Often the process symbolically changes us from one of these states to another, usually in a way that gets our lives flowing more than, or

---

[30]Those beings who exist outside the general consciousness generate more (starseed) energy than the general population or less (the regressive ones) energy than the norm. Often the latter exist as parasites on the lives of the former.

in a different direction than, before the transformative event.

With Taurus at the North Node, the Soul/Moon is taking in particles/structure and releasing energy from it at the site of the South Node. These are the investors in life; they invest physical resources in energy and power. They invest forests in housing, anarchy in societies, and old habits into a new sense of being and purpose. If there is not a sense of the continuity of life, there will be condemnation around some of these activities. Still, the essence of Taurus can be expressed as, "It's all good!"

These are the movers and shakers of society. They produce life and health for individuals, for society, and for the totality. The production of energy/power will be the theme of such lives. They can look like destroyers, but in the universal economy they are simply transformers. Always they change the status quo, releasing energy from the obsolete for use in the future. The focus may shift from personal to social to spiritual, but it will remain on transformation or reform or generating new life from the ashes of the old. One version of this is powerful leadership, either political or religious.

Such lifetimes can be painful, for it sometimes seems as if there is nothing that is sacred to the individual, nothing that may be kept and owned. If these cannot see into the depths and distances of life, they must learn to do so. Otherwise they are simple nihilists. Since they are often subject to criticism, the sense of self and mission must be strong. Natives with a Taurus North Node must accept this and trust that LIFE knows what it is doing in appointing *a time to be born and a time to die*. These people must also learn that the only real point of a large bank account is that of financing a period of life that is devoted to the beginning of a new developmental direction such as producing beauty or wisdom. Even gold will lose its value if it is not moving; i.e., if it is not being invested in something.

Social structures are temporary. Usually they have a longer life than the individuals who experience them, but in time each structure must give way to a newer, more modern, version of the principles for which they stand.[31] Certain social structures are disintegrating at this time. Two of these are organized religion and traditional marriage. The energy from these must be released for a new way of honoring life and its creator and a new way of relating masculine and feminine energy.

Spiritual structures are also temporary, but this is an abstraction that requires considerable spiritual maturity to grasp comfortably. The personal spiritual structure is the energy quantum that we call the core essence of self. It is what we mean when we use the pronoun "I." At some point even be-ingness changes and changes again. The simplest form of this is when we move our self-perception from form to spirit, when we realize that we are not merely a creation of Deity, but rather an off-spring destined to grow into maturity. The Scorpio North Node is taking in light and *stepping it down* into physical form. It is *destroying* its invisibility and making it visible. Form will be released

---

[31]This book is intended to teach new ways of expressing the ancient principals on which the structure of astrology stands.

at the Taurus South Node. These are lives of construction and creativity. They function on three levels: *building personal, social,* and *spiritual structures.* The point of dissolving any structure is to invest its energy into another structure and its lesson is that nothing is ever truly destroyed; it only changes form; i.e., it *transforms.*

At a personal level the Scorpio North Node seems intent on losing itself; this can take the form of some suicidal action. It will invest its life in sexual activity with the (usually unconscious) intent of dissolving the astral body by investing the personal energy aura into another person. Historically, women have been taught to seek such loss of individuality. To a lesser extent men followed suit.

Only at more advanced levels of awareness is this appropriate. We need, first, to have a solid self to invest. With more consciousness the intent will be to find another who functions at near the same vibratory rate and who will cooperate in the process of investing the two energy fields into a third *new* structure. In such unions the individuality of the participants is lost in the personality of the union. When the merger is structured appropriately, the process of returning to Source has begun.

Another version of this invests the personal life into some social structure. The most obvious example of this is the phenomenon currently known as a cult. Less intense versions include lives devoted to reform, especially political or religious reform. The third level is the life devoted to one's version of God. These are the nuns and monks of life who live disconnected from self and society in service to Deity.

In such instances, outlines of personality can lose boundaries and individuals sometimes become so nebulous as to almost lose visibility. One sees persons who are so fluid as to completely lose direction and sometimes form. The ultimate negative goal of such lives is that of becoming a sacrifice on some personal, social or religious altar.

The final state is the realization that we can, by our loving attention, influence the process by which these transformations take place. This begins with the magician who happily makes objects appear and disappear. When he gets past the idea of simple illusion and can manipulate the very life energy in magical ways, he is but a step from having control of his own manifestation in visibility and invisibility. Soon he will have conscious control over whether and when and where he incarnates. At this point the nodes fuse in typical Scorpio fashion.

Probably the *best* use of the fused axis is the fully conscious one. When this is achieved we can learn to merge and withdraw at will. This is pictured by the human sexual act, but when it is not under the direction of a conscious being, withdrawal is incomplete. The result is that one-or sometimes both—*continues to feed on* the other, even after physical separation. To regard sexual interaction as *merely a body function* is suicidal, particularly for the evolved. The higher our vibrations/level of consciousness rise, the more critical it is that the act be performed with full consciousness. This means that it must be performed with reverence and dedicated to the increase of life. By this we do *not* mean to restrict it to the procreative act. We refer to sexuality dedicated to the creation and maintenance of life, and more specifically *human* life.

At its broadest this axis will teach us that creative power is generated wherever a fusion occurs. These can be used in series to increase the power at the end of the series, i.e., to change the *voltage*. At this point the boundaries between the personal, social, and spiritual merge, and we achieve the mastery of power, becoming co-creators with our own Source. After this we will incarnate with a new nodal axis.

Leo-Aquarius

Where the Taurus-Scorpio axis is about formal, visible, physical structure, the Leo-Aquarius is about the recognition of the invisible spiritual structure of identity that creates, transforms, recreates, and sometimes transcends the physical one. Even as our physical body is *made by* our individual spirit, so also, our *spiritual body* is procreated from Original Being. We inherit our physical body from a human species and our spiritual body directly from unspecified Source of Life.[32]

Leo is ruled by the Sun. In chart readings we use the Sun to symbolize self, the physical father, and the personalized Deity that resides within.

Occasionally, Uranus, ruler of Aquarius, is called the *sun behind the Sun*. In the end we find that this represents the Greater Self that is our heritage and evolutionary goal. Certainly Uranus rules *acts of God*, and often, after the fact, we recognize these as times/places where grace steps in to readjust our lives and return them to their original alignment and intention. We might say that Leo refers to an individual or personal will/willingness/intention, while Aquarius refers to the group will/willingness/intention. While the latter may refer to social groups, when applied to lunar nodes, it must be seen as the will, willingness/intention of LIFE as a totality. When personal activity strays too far from the path by which life evolves through individuals, some crisis or *act of God* intervenes to make a course adjustment.

The Leo-Aquarius nodal journey is directed toward bringing the personal will into full alignment with the impersonal or transpersonal will. The result will be a consciousness that each of us is a manifestation, focus point, or channel for Deity. We become aware of ourselves as the ONE living as the one. This is the true meaning of the number eleven, which signifies Aquarius.

The simplest way to understand Leo is in terms of inheritance, for it is linked to the *name*, the genetics, and the property that we do or can or will inherit. The statement of the Master Jesus, "Unless you become as a little child, you cannot enter/inherit the kingdom of God," is a statement of the principle behind this axis. Religious dogma has almost entirely obscured its meaning. At the time the statement was made, and until quite recently, family estates usually passed to the oldest son. While that is not often a literal truth in today's world, it still has symbolic meaning.

We have long been accustomed to thinking of Deity as masculine.[33] From that perspective, those

---

[32]Our human heritage includes color of skin, hair, etc. Our spiritual heritage also has *color*; we call that version of color an astrological sign.

[33]We believe that this is largely because so many languages use the masculine as a generic term which not only

most identified with Source would be *male*. More important, the masculine is the catalytic force in any creative act. The feminine role is to provide the place in which the *seed of the male* can be gestated into a form that is ready to emerge into the world consciousness and society.

Whenever Spirit intends to create visible, tangible structures, its first act must be to provide itself with a *female*; i.e., a *womb* in which the *seed of the spirit* can gestate and/or a *channel* through which spirit can be transmitted, translated, transformed into some *solid*[34] structure. This, too, is a creative act, and intended to be realized as such. When it is, the feminine can claim equal inheritance with the masculine.

We caution readers not to get hooked on the idea of human gender, but to realize that we are using the terms in the abstract. *Male* spirits are outreaching/radiant energy. *Female* spirits are indrawing/magnetic energy. Each of us has both male and female elements in our makeup/chart. These are the polarized areas where we are alternating the experience of giving and receiving.

In each quadrant of the zodiac and of the house system, the third and final sign is a conscious one, both and neither male and/or female. The mutable signs may be likened to breath or to alternating current. They point to our dual spiritual structure, to the need to make both aspects conscious, and to the need to balance or harmonize them for the continuation of life.

This is the symbolic meaning of the Leo-Aquarius Nodes. The signs involved are feminine in mode and masculine in element and the axis depicts the ways in which the masculine and feminine forces relate.

Ultimately it points to a time when all people will be rulers of inherited kingdoms. Those who truly inherit the rulership of life must be *older children*; they must have evolved to a more mature state than they originally had.

On the nodal axis, Leo will always refer to our spiritual inheritance. Literally the Leo end is where we inherit and the Aquarius one is where we pass that inheritance on to our heirs, whether by blood, by adoption, or in consciousness. Leo is personal identity structure; Aquarius is non-personal (impersonal or transpersonal) identity structure. The balance and fusion is where our *I am* merges with the original *I AM,* which we call God. The path of the human spirit alternates between the personal and impersonal perspectives at several levels. The individual *I am* gradually evolves to a point where we are identified as the eternal totality being expressed through a *focus point* that we call our individual self. When our perspective shifts from the either-or to the both-and, in terms of man and God, we will have completed the Leo-Aquarius nodal journey.

The simplest way to understand this is to say that we begin the journey at Leo, with the understanding that we are the literal offspring of Deity, not merely its creation. At first we are *small chil-*

---

signifies males but *mankind* in general.

[34]This term has more to do with having sufficient boundaries to give shape and structure than its degree of solidity.

dren with a *limited world* and a correspondingly immature consciousness and view of life. We need the experience of wholly depending on the source of life which is called *faith* or *trust.* We *become (as little) children* to enter incarnation. Physically, this pattern continues for many incarnations, while our awareness gradually matures and we realize that we were *born* so that we might grow up to be partners, companions, and friends to our progenitors and teachers.[35]

The Leo North Node refers to the intake of spirit. More concisely we say that this North Node needs and gets conscious attention so that its formal spiritual structure or identity can remain alight/alive. If this if withheld—more accurately, if it is perceived as withheld—life will stagnate, the muscular structure will atrophy, and sometimes the physical heart will *break.* The physical Leo child must have love and attention, else Leo cannot remain centered in body. When that is insufficient, some very dramatic displays will be created to call attention to this need. When the spirit continues to starve into adulthood, the final drama can be a massive heart attack.

Leo North Node natives must consciously receive energy from their Source. The notion of inheritance must be understood to be a spiritual one, in which Spirit is infused directly from Deity. These are required, quite literally, to *seek, first, the kingdom of Heaven.* At earlier stages there will be a seeking for fame and recognition as the means of energizing self. In time, the ultimate source must be sought.

The Leo South Node is pouring out *light*/enlightenment or creativity. They create an inheritance for their descendants and/or for the *children of Earth.* These add much to the evolution of beings, society, or the general consciousness. Sometimes, by their works, more often by their beingness, they contribute to the evolutionary advance of life.

The Aquarius North Node receives enlightenment/genius/inventiveness and pours out new creation.

These beings are true co-creators, more linked to Source and sense of mission than to earth. The danger for these is too much detachment. There is a tendency to be so *heaven bound* as to be no earthly good. At earlier stages these seem hardly connected to earth at all. We would say that they, their spirit/energy, comes from another place, time, or dimension, and they sometimes have difficulty coping with earth.

The Aquarius South Node must release knowledge to the *group*, to whatever group in which it finds itself. The more evolved we become, the more directly we receive from Source, the more we can pour out that knowledge which attracts humanity into wholeness and back to Source. The intent of these nodes is to receive from Deity that which feeds the personal structure and pour out to Humankind that which feeds the species structure. There is always a sense of *role* or *drama* about these

---

[35]In the natural course of human development, the physical growth phase has always been the smallest portion of a lifetime. Some adults get fixated on this growth pattern to the extent that they refuse to learn beyond a certain age. In so doing they limit their capacity to evolve, but this is a choice, not a matter of natural evolution.

lives. They are the chosen ones, or they have volunteered for a special mission to life. That mission is to bring the emanation of spirit into the world so that all may be enlightened.

The synthesis and completion of this nodal axis will lie in the twofold realization that whatever we receive is ours only for a little while and must be passed on. In this sense we are but channels or conduits for spirit in its mission to create, recreate, light, and relight the light that creates life as an evolving path to greater life. This axis is about God-consciousness, and the realization that we are the gods and goddesses resident on earth, and that we do, quite literally, inherit both the genetics and the property of our Divine Progenitor. Usually we say that the Sun is the father and Leo is the Son. Jesus said, "The Father and I are One." He also said, "Ye are the light of the World."

He then went on to pray the magnificent prayer in John 14. If we read that as a lesson in consciousness, we will know the truth that will set us free. Full God-Realization and full Self-Realization will merge these nodes, and we will have achieved that state beyond which karma no longer has power. We will live with full choice as the gods and goddesses that we are.

Mutable Nodes

Mutable nodes breathe. Theirs is the alternating current that powers living systems. Cardinal energy is the catalytic energy that radiates from spirit/being. Fixed energy is the magnetic energy that constructs and maintains the visible/tangible structures in which life invests itself for self-knowledge. These symbolize the polarization of light into waves and particles. Mutable energy is the reunited light energy, perceiving, experiencing, understanding, and mastering life. The mutable nodes direct energy into the building of personal and impersonal consciousness. They signify one who is building and/or expanding awareness in self, society, or the totality. For each, the focus is on personal, transpersonal, or impersonal awareness.

The vehicle for expanding awareness is relationship. Mutable node natives will be developing or expanding the relationship with Self, with Others, or with the Totality. This will produce introversion, extroversion, or, in time, a good balance.

Anything mutable has multiple applications. Examine the chart to see whether the emphasis is on awareness of the being structure, the emotional structure, the physical structure, or whether the principle focus is the nature and function of consciousness. With that decided, look for supporting evidence to see whether the individual is more interested in learning experientially through relationships or through more traditional educational structures.

Gemini-Sagittarius

Gemini-Sagittarius deals with information processing as a function of consciousness. Gemini is the perceptive function. It also *names* objects, activities or other units of organization, such as lists and files. Sagittarius is the function that expands ideas through the attraction of details and related ideas or systems of thought, according to a structure of *language* and belief. Sagittarius can abstract the principle from the concept, and build the concept from principle. Gemini's focus is on rote learning. Sagittarius' focus is on understanding, conceptualization, and teaching.

At its simplest, Gemini may be considered a data base. It correlates to a physical toddler stage when much energy is expended on learning a stock of words that they may or may not understand. *Young Gemini North Nodes are not much concerned with meaning; they want and need to be seen and/or heard, to be recognized, and to have a name for self and everything in their world.* They also correlate with the Adam allegory, as he named all life.

At the next level children begin to formulate questions, and a true Gemini child may constantly disrupt Mother's routine with unending questions. When such mothers lose patience and enforce silence, it drives the questions inward. For some this results in shifting the perceptive function from a conscious information collector to a tuning device capable of searching the files of information available from the unseen realms of life.

Gemini questions create a vacuum that the next higher level of awareness must answer. If that awareness lies in the invisible realms, Mercury will evolve from intellect to a feeling function and begin to reach out through the lunar channel for its answers. At this point the planet Mercury will refer to the full spectrum of consciousness and not merely to intelligence.

Sagittarius is a far more complex consciousness. Gemini's words now have meaning and can be used to *calculate* other information. Sagittarius might be compared to a coprocessor that can expand or extend its own memory. As it evolves, Sagittarius works with larger and larger concepts, gaining increasing speed and range in its calculations. Always it is triggered by Gemini's need, by the questions asked. As the axis advances the questions get more complex and the answers more accurate and complete.

Traditionally, Gemini is the student and Sagittarius the teacher. In such terms the resolution of the nodal axis will be the realization that these are inter-dependant, for the teacher was once a student and will be again. Even so the student may once have been a teacher and will be again. This is a clearly revolving cycle in which we learn what we teach and, by teaching it, learn more. This text is an example of the process. As the author creates the teaching tool, even so she is taught by her guides who transmit much of it via her own channel.

Another example is the astrologer. Astrologers take in a data base of principles, but it is the application of these principles, time after time, to individual charts that really make them come alive. This is shown by the high incidence of Gemini-Sagittarius influence in the charts of astrologers and results in expanded consciousness for both the practitioner and the clients.

The Gemini-Sagittarius nodal axis is an evolution-class, regardless of the direction of energy flow. It probably alternates from one incarnation to the next, building consciousness step by step. The more we realize that the students teach the teacher as much as the teacher teaches the students, the more mastery we will achieve. This is part of the cycle in which logic ends in intuition and intuition produces new levels of logic.

At another level the Gemini sibling relationship is where we learn the principles on which we will base our later social relationships. Gemini teaches us to reach out to one another. Sagittarius teaches us that no one is entirely alone, each has extensions in consciousness; i.e., friends and family and that when one takes the hand of another, there is an extended effect as each will become acquainted with at least some extensions of the other. This is how society becomes integrated. In an abstract way it is also how individuals achieve integration. As you study the astrological principles, this is clearly illustrated, for we see that no single planet or aspect stands alone, but that each adds to or subtracts from others, either expanding, intensifying or sometimes contracting its effects.

The Gemini North Node takes in sensory information and learns from it. The Sagittarius South Node releases principles, belief systems, and concepts of meaning. This axis is about understanding what is learned and teaching it. This is the student of enlightenment and, in one way or another, the entire life is about learning to understand how life works, and what it means. Always these lives have significant meaning.

The Sagittarius North Node is the teacher of enlightenment. These people understand concepts and principles, and can break them down into their component ideas and applications, clarifying meaning. Their lives become a living explanation and illustration of the principles in which they believe, whether or not they perform the traditional role of the teacher. They are *translators*; they translate the abstract concepts into practical ideas. Their lives will be a living lesson.

Both are teachers. Gemini North Node usually teaches basics while Sagittarius North Node will teach more advanced courses. When the course of life is seen as cyclic, we realize that either may precede or follow the other. Often they teach in the realms of religion, philosophy, psychology, self-realization, spiritual growth, astrology, or another *occult* study. A common form of teaching is that done in the counseling professions.

The synthesis of the axis is she or he who constantly learns and constantly teaches. It is the teacher who realizes that she or he does it for self-learning and for the students. Good students *drive* teachers to higher and higher levels of self-realization. With these axes, the upward and outward spiral of evolving life is almost visible.

Virgo-Pisces

Virgo is ultimately hands-on experience. It is conscious, visible, physical activity designed to practice and use the individual spiritual, astral, mental or physical body in the service of life. Virgo has strong connections with the body and how it works/functions because it refers to solid, physical experience. Consequently it rules health and the work that we do. On the nodal axis it points to the body and physical life as the necessary vehicle for the development and use of consciousness.

When we understand that the body is a concentrated, stepped-down, quanta of spirit/energy, we will have many answers that students of enlightenment seek. Spirit *falls* in vibratory rate to become physical form. At the beginning of any incarnational journey, it is only *a little lower than the angels*. We call this rate Aries. As it moves deeper into incarnate form, the rate continues to drop until, in Virgo, form and basic (physical) consciousness is perfected; i.e., full-grown, and as solid as it will ever be. At the cusp between Virgo and Libra[36], a choice must be made. If perfection is realized, the choice will be to go on to higher levels. If it is not, there will be a return to Aries to *try again*.

As Aries is the beginning or conception of an individual *form* that is separate from but connected to Source, so Libra is the beginning or conception of a merged and bonded formlessness which is not different from the totality. This return to Source begins at zero Libra. Leaving Virgo, the vibratory rate begins to rise. If Libra feels unworthy, or fears to let the body go, it will rush back to Aries to re-begin the process of solidifying structure.

Pisces is no more solid than Aries, but is at the end of the process. At the end of Pisces, form is *lost* or given up to complete the merger with Source and a period of absolute stillness and rest which has been called Heaven, Nirvana, Paradise, etc.

As a conscious axis, Virgo-Pisces refers to the realms of the seen/solid and the (almost) unseen/intangible. The hands-on experience that begins at Virgo becomes increasingly automatic, requiring less and less attention until in Pisces it moves under the dominion of the autonomic nervous system and functions unconsciously and automatically. The peak of personal control is in Virgo where all is at choice. The peak of impersonal control is in Pisces where our lives are run by some unseen force that we are expected to trust. We may call that force intuition, instinct, God, or The Force, or by any other name, but we must understand that it is neither unconscious, insane nor irrational. In Pisces we need to understand that we know what we are doing even when that knowledge seems not to be ours.

Virgo North Node takes in formal experience. She or he does the work, heals the dis-ease, fulfills a function in life. This leads to a release at the Pisces South Node of intangible rewards. The effects of Virgo causes are Pisces rewards. This is the axis that has been interpreted by certain religions as a need to *earn* heaven. More accurately, it simply says that practice leads to mastery. Initially much attention is required. With practice, each accomplishment requires less and less attention. Anything that loses attention loses form.

The Virgo North Node is the mark of one on his or her way to becoming unconscious. When all that can be learned from life in a particular form has been learned, when all that entered awareness has been mastered to a point of functioning automatically, then the energy quanta known as "I am" will return to its origin, merging with the greater "I AM." Remember that the nodes travel in reverse from other chart factors. This points to the possibility of reversing their direction at any point, according to whether we *feel*[37] O.K. with our progress. It is we who choose to leave formlessness from Pisces or return to it at Virgo. It is at these nodal points that the choice is made but its effect will be a gradual process that makes it look like an earned one.

The Pisces South Node release must be taken for granted and trusted. We are required to trust the outcome of our service, understanding that our Heavenly Parent is happy with whatever gift we

---

[36]This is imaged by the sphinx.
[37]They are the *Moon's* nodes, and the Moon symbolizes our feeling structure.

bring. It accepts the little gifts of children in the same spirit and with the same approval as the large gifts of the master. It is as simple as believing that the sun still exists even when we do not see it. So, also, the unconscious Piscean parts of life.

Pisces North Node is a being on its way to becoming conscious. The Pisces North Node may not have a true sense of personal identity but will see self as simply instinctive, a (hopefully) higher animal. It will use the spiritual energy for physical purposes that serve the physical, mental, emotional, or spiritual self. Only in the very advanced can these nodes be expected to act as consciously spiritual. What others may call intuition, these will call instinct.

Natives are practicing the use and application of energy to physical structures. They are often hard workers, and during the Piscean age many have become more afraid of hell/death than attracted by heaven/life. They can be so pragmatic as to have no conscious spiritual faith.

Such beliefs, if continued for many cycles, contain the possibility of total regression to a point of dissolving the energy quanta that is the core identity of being. This is referred to, in the Christian Bible, as the final judgment.

Still, this is a mutable sign and always open to remembrance of Spirit and goodness. Cases of more than temporary soul regression are rare.

Virgo North Node is a priest/priestess, the Virgin (committed to no man) from whom the divine being will be born. Pisces North Node is Eve, mother of incarnate life. Pisces South Node is leaving Eden. Virgo South Node is entering it. In these nodes lie the realization that the Alpha and Omega, the beginning and the end, are in the same *place*. Astrologically that place is known as the space between Pisces and Aries. Socially, it is the place between Libra and Virgo. Each is a turning point, and at each there is a pause and a decision to be made. Thus the wheel of life pauses and moves on. Sometimes we think that we control it, but the only thing we really control is the speed at which we travel. Life will live us, whether we live it or not. That is our promise and we may choose to make it our hope or our despair. Once we leave Source we are committed to the journey until we realize it as complete, perfected and mastered.

The Nodal Axis in the Houses of the Horoscope

It may be that the house placement should be given more weight in interpretation than the sign placement. It is more relevant to mundane affairs, for it shows in what areas of life we attract attention/energy and in what areas we release energy/give attention to others. Much of the way we view this will depend on our beliefs and values and these are shaped by our personal evolutionary level *and* the environment in which we live.

The North Node area is where we are naturally *fed*. It is where those things that we need to support life come to us most easily. Very often it is where money or other resources arrive spontaneously and we are "lucky." North Node in the lower half of the chart usually refers to more visibility during childhood. In the upper half it defers the capacity to attract more than minimal attention/energy until later in life.

What happens at the South Node will depend on the level of awareness we have achieved, and that will usually change during a lifetime. The unconscious being will see the South Node point as an anus and consider the output to have little or no value. Such releases can fertilize other gardens but are of no further value to those beings who are getting rid of them. With this mind set, about all the gains that can be derived are more efficient methods of waste disposal.

At a slightly higher level the South Node release may be seen as progeny and the value of progeny will be judged by the level of self-worth. Occasionally progeny are mistaken for waste products, with some painful results.

The spirit/energy that catalyzes our lives is neither used up nor destroyed. Initially, the energy quantum, which we call our spirit, chooses to step-down its vibrations through the lunar channel/transformer to a rate that makes it visible on earth as a body. We accept the world-view that to be visible is to be tangible and by that acceptance we make it so. From that point we are a formal structure requiring a constant supply of attention to maintain its form in operating condition. We are like electrical appliances that must be *plugged in* to work. If those appliances are never turned on, if they are ignored or considered irrelevant to the activity of life, they will eventually deteriorate to uselessness. No more do we use up the energy we receive from the attention of those around us.

That which we receive we pass on to others. This is one reason for marriage and family.

Children must have attention. During the growth period all *feeding*—whether of food or attention—goes to growth of structure[38]. Every aspect of being is accumulating substance, intent on achieving adult status and entry into the life of the planet. This is the only point in life that appears to *use up* energy/attention. In reality, the energy is merely being stored as adult potential. The energy may be converted into structure, with some constriction of its motion, but it is not lost. Attention given to children is *never* wasted.

When attention is minimal and confined to the care and feeding of the body, we assume that physical food and its assimilation are the only things going on. When all we get (or think that we get) is physical food, we seem to release only waste. We do not see that these *wastes* are still potent and return to free energy when we forget them.

Approving attention from adults during those early years makes for stronger physical bodies with more integrity. Disapproval may also preserve life, but at a low level. Here the need to win approval keeps our attention on others and we give more than we get. If we are required to give a great deal of attention to the adults in our childhood we are preprogrammed to consider our lives entirely in terms of what we can give. This breaks the flow because we cannot receive. We seek anonymity and find meaning only in giving to and serving those whose lives we consider of more worth than our own.

Children need to be nurtured with approval. They must be valued/loved if they are to become stable adults. Those who manage to survive without adequate love or parenting only do so because of an ability to draw on some higher power/energy reserve. They may live on assets *laid up in heaven* in earlier incarnations or they may be fed directly from the invisible/heavenly realm by nonphysical beings who act as backup systems. Some of us have *partners* in the astral realm that made a joint commitment with us for service in this world.

The reality is that to remain physical enough (healthy enough) to accomplish anything in this world, whether it is our own self-realization or making some contribution to society or deity, requires attention/feeding from some source. The North Node points to that source.

At the next level the inflow is usually viewed as money. During the money experience we are offered the opportunity to realize that while money disappears from our personal lives, it does not disintegrate but goes on to supply the needs of others. Gradually we can begin to learn prosperity techniques. These point us toward total reliance on the constant flow of spirit/energy. We can learn total trust in the absolute supply that creates any reality we expect.

We will also learn—one way or another—not to hoard money in places where it cannot grow or serve some purpose. Certain investments are spiritually valid. *Burying* assets is not. Working capital and petty cash funds are fine. Putting money or other possessions on display as a proof of personal worth or value is not. No accumulation of possessions ever proves self-worth. Only activity that

---

[38]At this time, all the *bodies*, are being created/formulated: physical, mental, astral, etc.

contributes to the quality or quantity of life can do that.

From the house placement of the North Node we can predict the areas of life that will give to us most easily and graciously, provided that we pass that energy on through the South Node. Whatever form the energy takes, it will supply our needs if we let the energy received at the north flow smoothly and without restriction at the south. If we hold on at the south, our lives will become severely constipated, stop moving, and require some kind of purge if we are not to die a little.

When there are positive aspects to the nodes, the energy flow has support and assistance. It moves freely. At the mundane level the body experiences generally good health and the finances will be equally healthy. Usually the native can set and achieve goals at or above the norm for the general population of his or her time and location. When there are negative aspects to the nodal axis, there will be apparent hindrances that seem to slow progress and pull the native off-course. At more advanced levels of awareness these will be understood as resistance against which effort must be applied, sometimes resulting in greater accomplishment than might otherwise have been made. A few squares in a chart prevent boredom!

Still, squares are the most problematic because they affect both inflow and outflow. We may then view them as *shorts in our wiring* that *ground out* or sidetrack our energy. Later, with the squares resolved[39], that same point can act as a focus, similar to the positive use of a Yod. An example from my own life demonstrates.

My North Node is in Sagittarius in the second house South Node is in Gemini in the eighth house, and both are square Virgo Neptune retrograde in the eleventh house. The attention issue was confused from the beginning. I was taught to *perform in public* at an early age, but the praise I received was syphoned off by my mother. She needed it to *prove* her value as a mother/person.

Although I received considerable public approval, home was entirely different. One instance of getting approval from my mother and one from my father stand out so sharply in my memory as to suggest that these were the only such events that I experienced. I seemed never to do *anything* that was entirely pleasing to either. The need to win approval became a serious energy drain on my life for many years, damaging both health[40] and finances.

It also confused/Neptune my hopes and wishes/eleventh house by leaving them weak and unable to get conscious attention/Virgo. I wanted to teach, even as a child, but the thing that I would teach did not enter my life until years later. In the meantime, great portions of my earned income went down black holes generated by mates.

Resolution: At mid-life I began to study astrology and was drawn into professional practice soon after. When I began to charge for my readings, a channel opened and supplemental, intuitively supplied information funneled into each reading. The channel continued to grow, resulting in

[39] See our work on squares in *The Dynamics of Astrology*.
[40] Sixth house cusp is ruled by Neptune

the writing of books that pour through my consciousness from some *extraterrestrial* source. The hopes and wishes of childhood, deferred until the future/after completion of the tenth house are now manifesting. Notice that the future/Sagittarius has merged with the present/Gemini, with an output into the transpersonal realm of the eleventh house.

Whether positive, negative, or both types of aspects appear, the chart must be examined to detect exactly what is going on. Conjunctions to either node are especially problematical. Some represent energy drains, while others represent persons or circumstances that help, or sometimes drive, us to greater heights. Visualizations, affirmations, or rituals are appropriate in directing these activities.

A Mars square, for example, may waste much energy on anger, and a semi-square on frustration. Anger or frustration can be converted into a determination so that I or others will not have to deal with the kind of problems represented by the aspect. As we do so, the energy can be used as a power source to change the world or at least our part of it. Look to the sign and house placement of aspecting planets to decide whether they will spontaneously help or hinder goals, and apply the techniques above to redirect or enhance their natural tendencies. The higher/older signs are wiser, more mature, and less likely to be derailed by a negative aspect.

A trine-sextile adds comfort, again with varying results, from inertia to a steady flow of production. Inconjuncts and quadrates reverse polarity at some point in life, changing from hindrances to helpers. Sevenths and ninths show something *destined* or something that is specifically timed to occur at a particular point in life. These require trust more than effort. Intercepted nodes will not reveal their workings until later in life, almost always after the first Saturn return, often not until after the Uranus opposition, and sometimes not until the second waning square of Saturn to its own place, or the Chiron Return. These usually depend on transits or progressions of one or more outer planets across the interceptions for resolution.

Meanwhile, intercepted nodes disconnect the inflow from the outflow, diverting energy elsewhere. In time a major move in space or perspective will open the interception and reconnect the axis.

At the level of the ego, interceptions represent soul-wounds. Until the soul-wound heals, the energy received at the North Node will be diverted into compensating for or healing that wound.

It is relatively easy to find out whether our own energy is being syphoned off or side-tracked. When health or finances suffer, someone in our immediate environment is nearly always acting as an interference in the energy flow. This one can be a parent, or later in life, someone in a personal relationship with us who is a personification of the buried memory of the original energy drain.[41]

Because of this the nodal axis is regarded as significant in relationship or comparison charts. The planets aspecting our lunar nodes commonly represent actual persons and their relationships to us, including the energy dynamics that result from these connections. Since the natal horoscope is a

---

[41]A popular book, *The Celestine Prophecy* by James Redfield, has much to say about the dynamics of human energy flow; sixth house cusp is ruled by Neptune.

birth chart, the original persons represented will usually be parents, grandparents, or others with whom we spend significant time early in life, especially during the pre-verbal period. Sometimes forgotten events from this period will be *remembered* as repeating experience in adulthood so that we have the opportunity to deal with that experience on a rational level. This can be true of any aspect in the chart, but is especially true of those that contact the nodal axis.

It is important to realize that the first reading of any house placement is that we have been taught by our early environment to have a certain image, value system, belief system, and response system. We have been expected to fulfill a particular role in the family and to function in a particular way. We have learned to expect certain reactions to, and effects from our activity.

Later we will realize these same house polarities have a higher function as indicators of the ways in which we intend to express our inherent capacities. Our personal assets, our natural methods of communication and relating, and our role and function in life can be read. It is interesting to note that in some fashion or another those people who had the care of our childhood did sense the truth of us, whether or not they believed that truth to be acceptable, righteous, or useful. All the judgments that we learn to apply to self and others originate in the attitudes that surrounded us during our formative years. This is why we look at the psychological dynamics of a chart in the light of the house system.

Keep the laws of consciousness in mind. Remember that the feeding referred to is the attention received. Wherever/house and however/sign we receive attention as children, we will continue to give attention to ourselves. Attention is the means by which we hold mass in form; it is the *glue* that connects the atoms and molecules of form. Focused attention is creative. It keeps our bodies, our possessions, the structure of our lives, and even our world in form. Energy/attention received at the North Node is passed on at the South Node and used to maintain the structures of reality.

Often the nodal axis is split in the original environmental system. This does not allow a proper energy flow and its effect will be that of reducing the livingness of the child. This can produce frustrated, angry, sullen, and often ill, children because certain toxins that need release are being tightly held in the name of survival.

It is important to realize that this axis is an opposition, and like all oppositions must be treated as Libra-type energy. The two must be married, balanced, and perceived as equal, and they must share with each other. Any inflow is qualified by the outflow; any outflow is qualified by the inflow. We cannot give what we have not received; we cannot receive with full hands. This is the most significant lesson to be learned from the Nodes of the Moon.

The Nodes in the Cardinal Houses

The cardinal or active houses describe the way we learn to identify ourselves. They have a great deal to do with the *names that people call us*. They form the grid-work of our sense of self and its place in time and space, as we learn it from the adults in our childhood.

Like everything else in a chart, the houses have a spiritual meaning. The cardinal houses describe the ways in which we express or project our spiritual purpose in this time and place. Example: If I am (sun) a builder (Taurus), what I will build, the materials I will use and the availability of them, combined with traditional moral, philosophical, or religious judgements on building, or on my particular gender doing it, will all be a part of how I see myself and am seen by others. Individuals do many things with images. Some project strong ones, others almost none at all. Some images are clear while others are blurred by scars and fingerprints. A given individual may hide behind the image, use it pragmatically, only in crisis, and so on. . . .

When the nodal axis falls in the houses that create image, self-awareness becomes a critical issue of life. It will be the power-line which maintains a visible expression of the solar intent, showing which part of the image is most receptive and which is most expressive. The opposing axis will always have some effects of the square. How strong these effects are will be shown by whether and how close the aspect is between the nodal axis and the horizon or meridian that squares it.

When assessing the nodes in the image structure, remember the critical part that parents, or those who do the parenting, play in that image. For the infant, the Ascendant represents the forming definition of self, while the Descendant represents the forming definition of the not-self. The bottom layers of this image and reflection are both heavily overlaid by the mother. By her attitude toward both herself and her child, she sets the tone, in the deepest recesses of personality, for all the conscious awareness which will develop in the years of individuation. This begins in the womb and extends through the first few months of life with little or no interference. It might be likened to the footer which is placed beneath the foundation of a house. If it is mushy or cracked or uneven the foundation will suffer and that suffering will be passed on to the house and to its occupants in some form.

The fourth house describes our sense of security and *home*. It is the place where the identity is born into visibility. It is where the body is first exposed to the realities of life and where it first experiences the reality of a world in which other persons and things who are not-me exist. By implication the *birthplace* is the prime factor in the final goal. The fourth house describes the world in which the child learns what goals are available to members of *our family*. Hopefully, the mother or family will support, feed, pay attention to the child, helping it in successfully accomplishing its goals. Far too often, mother and family teach children that their only moral, legal, or possible goal is to support others in their needs, desires, hopes, wishes, dreams, or even in their dramas.

The social goals which the native is taught to set may appear to have everything or nothing to do with the goals of the spirit who is the cause and creator of the body. Still, what appears to be a hindrance often becomes the driving force for initiating real and powerful spiritual growth.

Cardinal nodes activate self-realization. This will be empowered by the process of individualization (first), socialization (seventh), something originating in the past (fourth) or in the future (tenth). The North Node energizes or drives the process; the South Node magnetizes, creates a hunger, or pulls the person involved into his or her pre-incarnationally-intended path.

Evolution through cardinal nodes culminates as centering in time and space. This is the absolute of God-Consciousness. It is the realization that I am not merely this *or* that. Rather, I am both this *and* that. It is the realization that what I was, I am and what I will be, I am. I experience myself as on a journey, but the reality is that all journeys lead to home. Much will depend on my attitude toward how I was taught to define home/family and my place in it. At first I have little choice about that; it is a matter of survival. In the end I am required to chose. That is also a matter of (spiritual) survival.

Nodes in the First-Seventh Houses

The first house is the way our ego is identified or named in the same way that our personal name or nickname and the face we present to the world described us. It describes the impression we make and the appearance we present.

North Node in the first grabs attention with its name and/or face. The attention received is derived from being a reminder of someone else. As a result the child tries to look and/or act as much like the original *from which it is copied* as is possible. This can be a positive or a negative event. The attention received may be praise, criticism, or some combination of both depending on the mood of the person giving attention, or even the response of more than one person to the image presented. It may or may not be pleasant to remind others of another. It never really helps us to know ourselves.

North Node in the seventh tries for attention by not-acting or not-looking-like some specific other. She or he may even attract attention as questions about his/her true heritage. "Where did this one come from?" is a common question. This child is often loved or hated by one parent because it does—and should not—or does not—and should—look like the other. Being a negative reminder of someone becomes a critical issue in getting enough attention to survive the childhood years.

In worst-case scenarios, natives with first-seventh house nodes survive to please one parent and spite the other, or because of the kind or quality of attention given by one and in spite of the kind or quality of attention received from the other. The child becomes the balance, the connection, the pivotal point of the parental marriage and the (sometimes only) subject about which they converse.

This child may develop a very strong or a very weak self-image. Sometimes the self-image replaces the ego image. Other times the ego image completely overwhelms the self-image. Remember that these are simply the two sides of the identity and usually at some point after adulthood is reached the two conjoin and begin to share the body in cooperation.

Until that time the adult seventh house South Node will release energy into marital relationships, or social enterprises or to some significant other because something about the choice reminds the native of the person who originally fed him or her. Usually this one will *marry the mother* in some sense and will support the mate in ways that keep the other dependant. More obviously, the seventh house South Node will attract a dependant, perhaps child-like, mate who overwhelms the native with its neediness.

With the South Node in the first house there will be a tendency to marry for self-image. This one marries because it allows him or her to identify as someone's mate and/or parent. This gives a reason for remaining dependant on the other for certain needs—either financial or emotional support.

First-seventh nodal axes set natives up for give and take relationships because they have not learned to share, lacking either a personal or a social image that is wholly their own. They predict a tendency toward compulsiveness about marital relationships. There will be a strong sense that either marriage or the single life are prerequisite to adult survival, at least to survival of the self-image. In reality, what is being preserved here is the ego image as defined by the Ascendant and first house, while what is being threatened is the true self, as defined by the Sun.

With these nodes, marriage will remain more adversarial than cooperative until the *inner marriage* takes place and the self unites with the ego. Many of us have been taught that the ego must be sacrificed to the self, but these nodes must learn that the ego is merely the form which the spirit/self takes. With this nodal axis, the Sun's house—where it shines most brightly—must take the shape of the first house. The light that shines in the Sun's house must be directed into the physical structure defined by the first house so that the native identifies with light as substance (seventh north) or substance as light (seventh south).

The spiritual goal for the physical plane then becomes the creation of an inner marriage that can express as an outer one. Conversely, the outer marriage will represent the inner to society. Whatever signs are involved, natives marry to *feed or be fed by* society. With full realization the nodes will balance at a point where they can breathe, becoming fully conscious of the continual energy flow between entities, whether single, multiple, or the whole that is the sum of all the parts.

Nodes in the Fourth-Tenth Houses

The fourth house is the *nest* into which we are born, the point in time and space where we emerge into the light. It is the outcome of any first house inception and refers to birth and rebirth. It describes our experience of home, and planets in it may describe the persons or attitudes that dominate the atmosphere which surrounds our earliest years.

This home continues to surround us for some years similarly to the way in which the womb originally did. The fourth house is our foundation in life, what makes us feel *at home*, conveying the emotional comfort of familiarity, whether or not it was truly safe. It becomes the question of feeling safe or unsafe as we move into adulthood. This context surrounds marital relationships because marriage puts us back into the feeling of family and home.

The tenth house is the extent of our original *leash*. It is what we learned to call the goal of human life, or our particular life. It is the place of greatest independence, not *old* age, but closer to *middle* age, or the peak and apex of life—a point of achievement. When we cross the Midheaven (experientially) we are on the return journey. This says nothing about the length or kind of journey, simply defining the point, in time, space, or consciousness, which opposes the starting point. In the opinion of those who surrounded our birth, the Midheaven describes how far we can go from the time/space of our birth.

The fourth-tenth nodal axis assigns energy resources and their availability to the area of feelings (fourth) and responses (tenth) and how we respond to our feeling base. When the fourth house home was not-safe, we may feel that we have to live in unsafe circumstances to receive adequate energy supplies (North Node) or to be able to release energy (South Node). Mundanely, the necessity for feeling safe or unsafe will act as a limit on our ability to evolve. The interesting thing about this axis is that it predicts a rebirth which can be achieved by changing responses first, resulting in changed feelings *or* by changing feelings/attitudes with a resulting change in responses.

The North Node in the fourth takes much attention in infancy. What kind of attention it gets and how much the kind or quality of it changed as the child began to develop more independence (learning to walk, talk, go to school, etc.) forms the foundation of the entire life. For better or worse, this North Node affects every area of life because we learn that our greatest safety lies in remaining dependant *or* in becoming increasingly independent.

It is important to remember that the fourth is the Cancer house. It is basic water flowing, moving, changing. It is also the most rapidly growing phase of life, so either node in the fourth receives an ego message to grow and change, usually for the entire life. Meanwhile, the Capricorn-flavored tenth house sets boundaries, defines success, imposes goals, and generally confines, inhibits, disciplines, or manages the flow, depending on the degree of balance.

One end of this axis constantly moves and grows like a live infant. The fourth house inflow will push out the limits of the tenth house outflow, forcing growth, often through explosive crisis. Even more critically, the tenth house inflow of limiting circumstances combined with a moving growing outflow will create an inner vacuum that will trigger an implosion. This axis is always about equalizing the pressure between childhood and adulthood, between dependance and independence, between birth and maturity, and/or between maturity and death/rebirth. It is simply an expression of the need to discipline or limit the influence of our foundations on our goals, and our goals on our foundations. The two must reach a balance so that we are centered in *vertical* space, living on earth, between the dark and the light, in that place where both can be seen, understood, and managed for our greatest comfort and accomplishment.

The energy dynamics of these nodes is particularly interesting. Increasing flow at the fourth house end nearly always produces a heavy buildup of repressed feelings at the tenth. This will then *upset* the nodal axis, taking the whole chart with it. This is the dynamics of rebirth, spoken of above. Whether we are being pushed too hard or pulled too hard, the increasing flow will lead to rebirth, usually through crisis. Astrologers can say with certainty that any chart with nodes in the fourth-tenth axis, near the prime vertical, predicts at least one *major* change[42] of direction during that lifetime. The chart actually re-polarizes.[43]

---

[42]Make a note of such placements on Solar Return charts. These pinpoint years of repolarization.

[43]This is probably what is being imaged by those who warn of the earth's *pole change*. There may be an actual

The fourth house North Node is probably the best or worst of the house placements. This child demands a great deal of attention during infancy, because she or he makes much noise. If the attention received is positive and loving, the child will develop a positive self-image and can mature successfully. As each goal is reached, a new one can be born. If it is negative, at some point a rebirth must occur if the native is to remain on earth long enough to achieve its life goal. The rebirth allows a literal new start on foundations laid consciously and intentionally. This usually involves some version of re-parenting.

A tenth house North Node native gets little attention as an infant. As the child matures it learns that its only hope of gaining parental approval lies in succeeding in some goal which does not really belong to the child. Usually these natives are expected to be the fulfillment of the goal of one or both parents. As adults they want to be in high-profile positions because they require the attention to feel secure.

With attention too heavily weighted in the future, the threat of failure often *hangs over the head* and the whole structure threatens to come down. The child's own natural energy flow is being directed by another or others. This must stop if life is to succeed in reaching any personal fulfillment. Again, this often *crashes*, reversing polarity and allowing the native to begin again on personally constructed foundations.

The first lesson of these nodes is that parenting is the primary influence on how well our life energy serves us in our personal and social goals. The second lesson is that if the original choice of parents does not serve us, we can choose again. We may choose to re-parent ourselves or we may choose to rename and redefine the parental influence. It is always appropriate to see our parents as Mother Earth and Father God, for we are forever the offspring and inheritors of both human and the divine characteristics.

A fourth house North Node wants attention/feeding in private. It needs a secure home as a place in which to re-energize. It must build a safe, secure *nest* before it can begin its spiritual journey because it will be that secure haven which energizes future ventures.

This *home base* can be physical, emotional, or spiritual. Foundations can be regarded as personal—a physical *house* in which to live. Alternatively, they may be regarded as emotional—a need for emotional security, often mistakenly defined as having someone to nurture or be nurtured by. The third alternative is the spiritual foundation which can ground us in reality or keep us up in the air.

The tenth house South Node must release energy into some goal if it is to get any more. No matter how safe and secure that home base may feel, we must extend ourselves beyond it, if our life is to have any value or meaning. In terms of life, the purpose of the child is to grow into adulthood, leave home, and then establish a new home from which new goals can be accomplished.

The means of *leaving the nest* usually, but not always involve some physical movement. If we regard

---

reversal of the magnetic poles, but the real change is one of choosing a new end-goal for humanity.

ourselves as a consciousness, leaving home could be a matter of publishing. If we choose a convent or monastery, leaving home may refer to some version of mental, astral, or spiritual *travel*. Always, if there is hoarding of the energy received, the flow will be hindered and eventually stopped.

A tenth house North Node refers to getting attention by being independent, goal-oriented, and/or mature. It may defer parental approval for a long time, or it may require the child to take care of the parents to get it. When energy enters from the tenth house, the release will be in the fourth. Even in childhood these natives are responsible for themselves and get or keep energy through taking care of themselves and/or others. At its most simplistic, the tenth house North Node must produce children and carry on the family name or traditions to get parental approval.

Literally this axis is about the effects of parental approval. If that approval seems negative and inhibiting, the simplest method of getting life moving is by choosing new parents. This means shifting your perception of *where you came from* to some place or idea other than a physical mother/womb. Change your origins so that you begin with a personal or impersonal intent, or even from your own earlier self. It is far easier to pick new *parents* than it is to change the ones you have. It is easier to create a supportive relationship with another source and example than it is to remake the ones you have.

At its highest expression this nodal axis will take you off the karmic wheel, allowing you to choose your own causes and your own destiny. This will allow a new personal image and new relationships. It will let you begin again as many times as you like until you *get it right*, or acquire as much experience as you like. Finally, it will allow you to see that the beginning and the end are the same, that we all eventually go home again and that we all, inevitably, succeed in achieving our goals. Literally, earth and incarnate life are on the plane between. We are always on our way in or out. The end is not the goal. Only the journey from goal to goal is. Wherever we are is where we must start. We get nowhere until we take the first step out the door.

In one form or another, this is the lesson of the fourth-tenth nodal axis. It requires us to live *centered in space* between our *birthplace* and our goal. It teaches us to be here now.

Nodes in the Fixed Axis

In the fixed axis we understand that we have formed a particular structure that will remain visible for a while. With the realization of life as form comes the passive mode. A *fixed form* of life retains structure temporarily out of inertia. It stays fixed only to the extent that it receives energy for its maintenance. While the cardinal nodes are active at both ends, having intent involved in both the intake and outgo of energy/attention, the fixed nodes are passive and magnetic at both ends. Both the inflow of energy and the outflow are directed toward formal/visible/tangible structures and their needs. To simplify: Fixed nodes direct attention to the need for formal structure at any level of manifestation whether visible or invisible.

Generally, a hindrance to the North Node from negative aspects will rob the individual of personal energy and the health will suffer. Correspondingly, inhibiting South Node release will steal creative abilities and limit the supply of supporting substance, money or other things that we need. Assistance, as trines, sextiles, and sometimes quintiles and deciles, will enhance the health of our bodies and life circumstances.

Nodes in passive houses are being directed, according to the time-space environment, toward the establishment and/or maintenance of some formal structure of life. We learn that we are (in) a body, and that this body has certain survival needs. At some further point we learn that needs evolve over time, according to our maturation rate. The general consciousness requires us to enter incarnate life as an infant, and declares that infants have certain needs that we learn to receive, create, transform, or transcend through the structure of this incarnation.

There may be an infant, a child, an adolescent, or some level of adult spirit/consciousness in and/or creating that infant body. This can seem to misalign the physical needs and the spiritual needs. When the nodes are in the passive houses, for that incarnation the physical needs take precedence over the spiritual until awareness that there can be no conflict between physical and spiritual rises to the surface of awareness.

The nodal purpose of placement in passive houses is to realize that needs can and do change their priority over time and/or according to the level of awareness we are currently expressing. These nodes refer to consciousness directed, by the environment, toward formulating, creating, reforming, or recreating suitable structures.

Nodes in the Second-Eighth Houses

Traditionally, the second house refers to our physical assets, beginning with a body and extending to possible uses for that body. It also suggests that we need that body, and must have certain things if it is to survive. By sign it may tell us which body—physical, mental, spiritual, astral—is our primary asset, most in need of feeding, if the others are to survive. Metaphysically, this most valued body is the place where energy is most needed for maintenance of its form and structure.

Mundanely, the second house defines the body and its needs: i.e., food, money, and moveable assets. Because all needs are met at the metaphysical level, it also represents what we do have/ own as a physical birthright and can claim as our spiritual inheritance. Usually this means the necessities of physical life. For the child these are food, clothing, shelter, and care. For the adult, these are money and other possessions that can be converted into the necessities of life. More accurately, the second house supports and maintains the first house image.

The second house North Node child has the attention of at least one adult who *needs*[44] the child to get their own needs met. In some way the adult draws attention/energy through the child. This child represents self-image (as a parent), or surety for a marriage and its assets. At least one parent will claim the attention of these natives, by right or need, far into adulthood.[45] This attention

---

[44]Remember that we are speaking of an ego program or learned belief that has no objective reality.

[45]This occurs when the child is physically, emotionally, and consciously emancipated from the possessing parent.

drain remains until the parental hold is broken, until true maturity is achieved. Independence is a birthright. The assets of this life belong to the spiritual mission for which it was created. As adults we have no right to permit the assets of our mission to be stolen by energy thieves.

The second-house North Node is a personal asset, brought over from other incarnations. From birth, these natives will be able to attract sufficient attention for survival. Negative aspects can drain some of it, causing energy depletion. There can be illness, especially of the energy depletion variety, but death will not result. At some point the nodes will merge and the entire axis will be transformed. With the energy leakage stopped, productivity may be incredibly high.

Remember that consciousness is rising in and through the value system, so money will be a real issue. When the value of the North Node energy intake is recognized, it will merge with the self-image. Self-worth will rise and a corresponding rise in income will result. Literally, the needs of the spiritual goal will be the greatest personal/physical asset of the life. The body will be maintained expressly for the use of the spirit. In exchange, the spirit will provide the physical needs. Jesus spoke of this when he taught his disciples to exchange their burdens for his yoke. He said that his yoke was easy and his burden light. With this axis we are allowed to ignore the ego needs entirely and focus on the spiritual ones. Knowing that the spirit needs a body, we can trust spirit to take care of it.

The eighth house refers to nonphysical assets, beginning with the soul/channel through which spiritual energy is received. In some sense it refers to the mother's possessions, which may later be symbolized as the mate's possessions. In the ego program the eighth house suggests that the needs of others are in opposition to our own needs. It implies that others (adults) control our possessions while we control theirs. The simple primitive logic of a child sees ownership and control as opposing forces. This is often begun and reinforced at the time of toilet training when the child is expected to give up the only thing which it can create, to some adult, upon demand. With threats and praise attached to this, it becomes a major source of energy production, setting up the adult who will emerge from this childhood for situations in which coercion triggers energy production. Reinforcement is added when the child is rewarded with food, setting the native up for weight and elimination difficulties.

The eighth house suggests that the soul must have certain things if it is to survive and that it must survive if the body-spirit connection is not to be broken. By sign, it can tell us how the soul/lunar channel empowers the physical life.[46]

Ego logic says that if the second house contains my assets, the assets of the eighth house belong to a significant other. Childhood's significant other is some adult, usually mother. Adulthood's significant other is usually a mate or some type of partner. As a result the eighth house becomes unowned assets that may or may not be controlled by the native. They will certainly be unavailable until the child reaches adulthood. They are also what we expect to receive as marital property.

---

[46]The eighth house is a Scorpio house and like anything else in Scorpio fuses with its polar opposite. This nodal axis will fuse and the life will be transformed as a result.

When North Node is in the eighth house we learn that whatever attention we get must be won or stolen from another. It may also refer to unpleasant or unwanted forms of attention. Still, we must have it to survive, so we are in a no-win place where the price of survival is too high. As a child, this native is a possession of the adults and its energy supply is, at least partly, sacrificed to their control. This may mean that an adult exists as a parasite on the child, in which case the child may be chronically ill or die young. It may also mean that the child is required to channel some or a great deal of energy into protecting itself from the adult(s). Until this is realized, that energy pattern will dominate adult relationships. Adult natives get, as a marital asset, someone who appropriates their personal assets. This drains time and energy for defense or replacement.

Constant drains equal soul coercion. They compel the soul to channel increasing levels of energy down them from birth. If the drain is removed, the need for a replacement will be felt as a lack of home or security. How the native truly feels about Mother will strongly color later marital relationships and determine the capacity for fulfillment in them.

Because sexual arousal creates a bond of the same type as that experienced by the infant with its mother, sexual liaisons contracted unconsciously trigger health problems and financial difficulties. An unhealthy mother-child bond will be re-experienced as sexual impulsiveness or compulsiveness which propels or compels the native into too much or too little sexual activity for the comfort of the body and/or soul. Therefore, the energy flow signified by the nodal axis will be derailed into physical reality until the soul wounds that are the origin of these problems are healed. One of the major difficulties in this is that the eighth house often holds secrets, or denial. It can point to places where secrets are being held or denied. For an astrologer, the eighth house can be a major source of information, allowing one to see deep into the soul.

Always the goal of this axis is the realization that our seeming liabilities are assets.

Physical experience maintains and heals the soul. From our soul resources comes the power to maintain and heal our physical life structures, the body and its support system. In the end, body and soul merge into a single entity both receiving from the Source Spirit and giving to that Spirit. The Master Jesus once said that "whatever you do for the least of these my/your brothers and sisters, you also do for me" . . . and . . . " I and the Father are one." You and your Source will be one—one being with joint ownership of all the energy assets of life. The Earth experience is about seeing this symbolized in form.

In the mundane sense, when we form a true and conscious union with another, we each invest our assets—not in the other—but in that third entity which is the union itself. As much as we invest ourselves in any union—whether physical, emotional or spiritual—so *in the union* those assets will draw interest, multiplying tenfold, a hundredfold, a thousandfold, or more. It is important to realize that no investments are permanent and uncancelable. There is always the option of removing our personal assets and investing them elsewhere for greater or different profit.

The natural trend is for the second-house North Node to provide personal, inherited, or earned assets. Eighth house North Node assets come from others in the form of inheritances or gifts, or is the interest accrued from mutual investments with a mate, partner, or group. The eighth house North Node may provide through insurance, tax refunds, spousal pensions, divorce settlements, tax refunds, etc.

In the spiritual realm, investing energy always leads to exponentially increased profits. Any energy, by any name, in any form, will multiply in this way. This is the ultimate lesson of the second-eighth house nodal axis.

Nodes in the Fifth-Eleventh Houses

The fifth house refers to our role in the family and to how we are taught that we should or do act. Action always involves risk, so it includes gambling. Because it is the expression of the Sun/father, it includes the idea of inherited talent or genetic structure, the place where we radiate or shine. Because we shine most brightly when we get the most attention, it includes romantic liaisons, which turn up the light that we have. If the North Node has a home placement, it is here, for the fifth house is about getting attention/energy and/or what activates our creativity.

The fifth house North Node child attracts attention by being talented, active, dramatic, by risking the reactions of the adults. She or he gets attention by expressing some aspect of at least one parent. To get approval she or he must play his or her assigned part or role in the family. How well she or he performs will be critical, so whatever this native does—whether success or failure—must be larger than life. It is as though the whole world is watching, and those watching eyes energize the performer.

Whether the self-concept is that of a winner or loser—and it must be one or the other because they get a thrill from taking chances, is extraordinarily important. These are the star-children, inheritors of the kingdom, and their natural heritage is joy. Their highest expression lies in being in love with life, acting from childlike innocence. Negative associations are anathema to these, causing the light to dim and creating great dramatic expressions of anger or gloom.

The eleventh-house South Node refers to a release of crisis, knowledge, change, evolutionary impulse, and/or entertainment of an audience. By their example they inspire others to hope, to wish, and/or to know, and the result of these is creation. Everything given at the fifth house will be returned from the eleventh, for this is the place where energy layers and accumulates, converting knowledge to action, and making hopes and wishes come true in form.

The eleventh-house North Node attracts attention by being unusual, by adapting, by transcending circumstances, or sometimes it makes the acquisition of energy a hope or wish that cannot be fulfilled until some future time. These natives get very little individual attention, and none based on personal assets or performance. In the family drama they are the supporting actors and stage hands in another's play. Seldom noticed, they get neither approval nor disapproval during childhood. Such energy as they receive comes from applauding or approving another's actions. They are required to go along with the program and not make waves or draw attention to themselves.

By doing so, they may not receive attention/energy, but at least what they have will not be taken from them. Quite literally, their real energy source is extraordinary—extraterrestrial—divine—or simply intangible.

Eleventh-house North Node people may hope or wish for parental approval, but must realize that this will probably not come. Instead they must learn to approve of themselves and to stop ignoring the extraordinary amount of approval that comes from friends, acquaintances, or groups. More than that, the amazing creativity that is the output from these nodes will affect the world for generations to come. They may not be as wealthy or famous as their counterpart fifth-house siblings in consciousness, but they will have a nearly unlimited and perpetual effect on the evolution of life. The highest level of eleventh house North Nodes is inspiration. If that inspiration is poured into creative output, inventions and art result. For some, the study and practice of astrology or other universal ideas will create personally valuable resources.

The synthesis and balance of these nodes come from realization that creation and evolution are two sides of the same coin. Incarnate life was created for the personal, social, and spiritual evolution of life, in all its many forms. It is the manifest expression of the glory of God. It is the place where our spiritual heritage evolves into higher and higher levels of being.

Nodes in the Mutable Axis

Remember that the nodal axis is about energy intake at the north and outflow at the south. What that energy does most naturally is shown by the sign polarity. How that is modified by our environment on earth is expressed by the house placement of the nodes. Cardinal houses teach being. Fixed nodes teach having. Mutable nodes teach doing. If the nodes are in mutable houses, we must do something to get the attention we seek. Doing takes energy so the expenditure of energy gets attention/energy and there is breathing going on at both ends of the axis. Mutable house placement of the nodal axis speaks of being rewarded for application and effort.

At the abstract level these nodes are about learning to function on the earth and about understanding the function and purpose of living on earth. Through this experience we increase our awareness of the relationship between the conscious and unconscious phases of life, as visible or invisible from the earth perspective. We learn about our relationships to time and space. In time we learn to balance between the visible and invisible worlds so that we can function in either at will.

Anything in a mutable context displays two or more faces. Therefore, each mutable node will divide and/or multiply its applications during a lifetime.

Nodes in the Third-Ninth Houses

The third house is about sibling relationships, short journeys, everyday tasks, and elementary education. It is the point from which the power to manage our lives originates, for our ability to communicate and perform simple functions is elementary to later development.

The third-house North Node child sometimes gets too little attention because there are too many siblings or because there is one sibling too close to his or her age. Attention is divided, as with twins. She or he gets attention by staying close to home, going away only short distances or for short periods. The thing that gets most attention, and the timing of that attention, is elementary education, or performing mundane tasks. Rewards are proportional to effort applied, so the ego may be invested in struggle or in keeping the home in perfect order. This is the child whom one or both parents talk to or about, think about, and often worry about.

When there is not enough attention from others during childhood, these natives may spend a period totally focused inward, making them seem alarmingly introverted. Still, if left alone, when the time for introspection is completed, the native will emerge into the world far better equipped than most around him/her expect.

With the ninth-house South Node, it is expected that what is learned will be passed on—tomorrow or someday. There will be a high focus on teaching elementary subjects, both educational and everyday skills. As adults, natives prefer the company of persons whom they perceive as having something to learn from them. The reality is that the more we teach, the more we learn, *if* we are willing to learn from our students. In this way, learning and the accompanying energy supply are available for the long term. The common difficulty is that the adult beliefs become a boundary on the learning process that makes these natives determined to teach their students to remain students who memorize much but understand little. This placement is largely about rote learning, which will not manifest any real output until the future, sometimes deferred to another incarnation.

At best these are the nodes of one who is learning a new perceptual function or a new basic principle of living. She or he is a seeker of higher and higher realms of consciousness. If such natives choose to alternate between learning and teaching modes, the upward spiral will expand and expand. The synthesis is that teaching is a path of learning, and learning is an adjunct to teaching. This allows easy breathing at both ends of the nodal axis and has the potential for space travel.

These nodes often produce a mathematical mind that takes the numbers or names learned in the third house and calculates answers or conclusions in the ninth. Such natives will often find that the conclusions reached have little meaning for siblings and peers but will bring wisdom, praise, and honor from those foreigners who will learn from him or her.

The ninth house is where family relationships are extended by adding in-laws. It includes long journeys in space, time, and/or consciousness as we travel in body and/or experience things for the first time. Concentrated attention comes from doing things that the parents aspired to but did not accomplish. These include higher education, travel, teaching, and the study of religion or philosophy. The timing range is high school, college, or even graduate school. Education is intended to take the native a little higher or farther than might otherwise be expected in members of the family or community.

As the third-house North Node implies divided or too little attention, so the ninth-house North Node implies multiplied, or too much, attention, or attention that stays focused on the child for too long—great expectations. Everybody sees this child, likes or dislikes this child, but there is no intense bond with anyone. She or he can feel like a stranger in a foreign land, struggling to understand the local laws, which seem to make little sense to him or her. The major focus of attention comes from crossing limits, breaking new ground, being a spokesperson or advance-person for the group. During childhood, the highlight of attention may be a runaway child, but when the event is over, that child may feel forgotten until she or he runs away again. In other cases the attention received is so severe as to limit the ability to travel far into adulthood.

It is understood that something is expected of persons with a ninth-house North Node, but they do not know what. Still, those expectations will shape the native's life, producing a seeker, searching for something unnamed. What we are expected to understand without question or explanation leads only to questions or the search for its name in adulthood. We are focused on trying to learn what/why we are expected to believe.

The third-house South Node need to question, to learn, and keep on learning will eventually set the individual free to pursue personal goals. The last hurdle in the way of successful emancipation is ninth house beliefs, imposed as absolutes, during childhood.

If the community—for this native is more a member of a community than of a family—expects failure, failure results. If it expects success, success results—but only in *communal* terms. Natives usually experience few feelings of success or failure. They simply have more questions until they move across the boundaries of childhood to a new foreign place with a new language, culture, or way of life as a framework or reference point from which to think. Even something like learning astrology, music, or computer language can energize the ninth-house North Node, setting the native free to become that which the heart desires.

As children these natives could receive concentrated attention from significant others only by running away, physically, mentally, or emotionally; but the third-house South Node doesn't take them very far. Always they come back home, to venture out again, and again, and again. Too many things, too many people, call these people back. They seem to be on a short tether, with only a little freedom, a little room to expand, until that day when they realize that the future is now, and that the past must be left behind.

The ninth-house North Node gets most of its approval in high school or college or even graduate school—sometimes by studying religion or philosophy, or through travel or sports. Depending on the community definition of the ninth house as travel, higher education, or sportsmanship, the native will find self traveling the community, teaching, or playing the game, without much personal meaning or passion attached. She or he does what is expected, but does not understand why—why she or he does it or expects it, or just why. Often the native becomes increasingly frustrated, sometimes jumping the fence, only to be driven back into a socially acceptable lifestyle, by guilt.

Attached to this area is a sense of promise that tomorrow or someday the child will get the attention she or he needs for self. Always there is an expectation of reward sometime. This can keep the energy flow at a low level, without much force or power for a long time. This is because the channel is shallow or hasn't enough drop to produce much due to the lack of passion and intentional direction. Any real feeling of achievement is often deferred until very late in life, when the native discovers that grandchildren or great-grandchildren love to hear the stories she or he has to tell. These stories of the native's travels and new experiences are a legacy to the future. Children learn from the elder sages of the tribe, and that is what this nodal axis truly describes.

The adult ninth-house North Node draws energy from an extended family, from travel and/or beliefs and/or from finding answers to common questions. They become counselors, teachers, ministers, or travel agents. They are natural translators of the spiritual concepts into their practical everyday applications.

The third-ninth nodal axis is about the fluctuation of energy that occurs naturally during the many cycles of life. How far we may travel before we need to change those boundaries and what or who determines our rate of progress is described here. In this house we learn to center ourselves in time, to be in the present, allowing the push from the past to balance the pull of the future. It is about traveling at a comfortable, easy pace and letting us develop at our own rate.

When the axis shifts to the social or transpersonal we are required to learn the same lessons in the context of increasingly larger groups—pairs, families, communities, countries, planets, etc. It is important to realize that this axis is mutable and has many applications. Only the principles are eternal, the applications vary from day to day, from year to year, from incarnation to incarnation. These nodes focus energy flow into (usually) an upward spiral; they say nothing about *which* spiral. Here we deal with time, as a function of our own progress. Time is not an absolute. It depends entirely on our perception and understanding of it.

Nodes in the Sixth-Twelfth Houses

The sixth house is the domain of work, health, and consciousness in form. It is an earth house so refers to solid reality. It is mutable, therefore conscious. Body consciousness refers to how the body functions, its health, how it works, and the work that it does. We refer to internal and external function. If the body is healthy, it works well. If it is unhealthy, it does not.

In childhood, the primary focus of attention was on how well the body functioned or served some purpose—its usefulness.

Included was the question of whether the purposes of the being who inhabited the body were being served or being made to serve the purposes of those who had control of it. The ability to function in society is established during childhood and affects the entire adult life. To the degree that the personal purpose and the family purpose do not interfere with each other, the energy will flow into and out of the physical form, resulting in good health and good work. When the body functions easily and well, it contributes to the continued evolution of being. When it does not, simple survival needs deplete attention/energy.

Sixth-house North Node children get attention by how well or ill the body functions and/or how useful they are to at least one parent. Other factors show whether the health is or is not good and for what the parent wishes to use the child. Any version of this can either deplete or energize the native and/or his/her life.

The critical issue is that the sixth house is the domain of consensus reality. Consensus reality is primarily focused on the solidly physical and tangible world. Notice the general belief that we survive on/by our work. That is how we get money and how we earn salvation.

Sixth-house adults function, use, or work on these same issues, bringing them to consciousness where they can be mastered and forgotten in the twelfth. Sixth house issues are very noticeable and get a lot of our attention. Twelfth house ones are (or should be) taken for granted, forgotten, unquestioned, unanalyzed. A sixth house North Node must work to get sufficient attention/energy to survive. Many of these individuals struggle for health or money for most of their lives without noticing where their time, resources, or energies are going. It is easy to steal from these because they have no personal interest in intangible results. Often they are considered too trusting or poor money managers because they are more interested in what they are doing than any side-effects of doing it. Their concerns are immediate, in the here and now.

Similarly, the twelfth-house North Node forgets or does not notice the need for attention.

Some take it for granted. Still, the output of work and healing ability in the sixth house can be seen, so the North Node inflow can be inferred from the South Node outflow. This individual lives unconsciously, by instinct, by faith, or in trust, or simply without knowing why. Where trust, faith, or reasons are placed is shown by the sign and house of Neptune, ruler of Pisces. These people may not notice any intuitive abilities, but seem to function from instinct or reflex.

The twelfth house child may be almost invisible to parents and family. Often they are forgotten children, required to find or create their own resources, while still so young that the Original Parent/Source[47] automatically steps in to care and provide for the child. Their dependence on invisible sources begins so early in life that it does not occur to them that everyone else does not live in the same way. How this manifests depends on the evolutionary level of the sign.

Some natives are so much in the background of their families that they do not learn marketable work skills. Other times they are heavily programmed to believe that having a job is immoral.[48] Some become dependent on society or on charity, drawing their energy from institutions. Other, more evolved beings seemingly drift through life easing over, under, or around obstacles in miraculous ways. They know the secret of life; they are that secret in form.

Most never notice how they function, but others will. Some criticize or condemn their methods.

---

[47]Consider the Biblical phrase "only begotten Son of God"—which has been reinterpreted "begotten only of God."

[48]This once included the vast majority of women who were *morally bound* to function exclusively as wives and mothers. Another example would be an individual born into some version of a ruling class.

Others follow them, for the pleasure of being in their aura, or the puzzlement about whom and what they are, or why they function as they do. Until the general consciousness rises to somewhat higher levels, most of these questions will remain unanswered. Still the axis represents an essential realization that practice leads to mastery, and true[49] forgiveness leads to healing.

A mature twelfth-house North Node was probably what caused the whole world to follow a man named Jesus who came to raise the consciousness of millions and to miraculously heal many, even raising some from the dead. Astrologers may not see many of these. They are the answer to the questions of the ages.

---

[49]True forgiveness means letting go the need to fix, justify, change, or get even. It means to walk away, giving the matter no more attention.

Nodal Returns

Nodal Cycles are 18.5 years. At hemi-cycles we notice attention received and others notice attention given. A balance of attention permits progress to the next level. An imbalance leaves us off balance during the next cycle.

Demi-Return, 9.25 Years

Grounds you in form; survival. Survival always has first call on our attention. If lack of approval keeps survival uncertain at the midpoint, it robs energy from the latter half of the cycle, interfering with our ability to fit-in socially. We cannot have a career, but must make do with jobs that finance survival.

First Return, 18.5 Years

Holds up a mirror for developing self-image; social visibility. If our place in society is still dictated by survival needs, we fade into the masses, unable to establish a personal place in the world. In essence we lose touch with our spiritual heritage and become servants in our Father's house and divine heritage.

Second Demi-Return, 27.75 Years

Grounds us in society, establishing usefulness; adjustments are made by Uranus trine Uranus and Saturn return (ages 28 and 29.5) These should create a sense of individual mission. When they do not, we cannot establish our rightful place in the world. During the late twenties, we may trigger a crisis intended to sever us from the past. This allows us to begin again on our own terms, or to make a new attempt to comply with the established terms.

Second Return, 37 Years

A new Jupiter cycle begins at age 36, setting a hopeful tone for this hemi-cycle. It is about expanding whatever was established at the beginning of the cycle and enlarging our sense of purpose—or purposelessness. The Uranus Demi-Return between ages 37 and 42 is a time of review and evaluation. Have we fulfilled our hopes and wishes? Can we still make the changes needed to do so? Is there a better way?

Third Demi-Return, 46.25 Years

Preceded by the Saturn Demi-Return, near age 45, this cycle naturally sets established patterns into unconscious habit patterns, for the last two decades of our careers. By the next Jupiter return, age 48, we may begin to look forward to the freedom to pursue travel and/or spiritual growth. Alternatively, if we are still at struggle for essential needs, depression may set in and Jupiter may simply overwhelm us with disappointment. Then the Uranus Quincunx at age 49 can trigger a second adolescent rebellion. This may look funny—meaning undignified—but it can also gain us the freedom that we wished for at the previous Jupiter return. Because Uranus often uses a very sharp knife to separate us from our restraints, this can look like a major loss—perhaps the loss of a career. At about this time our Chiron Return completely reorganizes our thinking for the task ahead. In women it often parallels menopause, graduating us from motherhood to grandmotherhood.

Third Return, 54.5 Years

The last half of this cycle can produce widely differing events. Some will use the next decade to wind down the concluding cycle. Others will be in the planning phase for the next cycle. Some will take early retirement at the second Saturn Return, age 59.

Fourth Demi-Return, 63.75 Years

For those who retired at 59, the goals of the next phase are taking shape. For those who will retire at age 65, it is still in the planning stages. Much will depend on how well the nodal axis is balanced. For some, retirement is an end. For the aware, it is a beginning. Free of social demands, it is meant to be a time of personal fulfillment and rapidly rising consciousness.

Fourth Return, 73 Years

For those who have achieved enlightenment, this can be the high point of life. Free from social demands, creativity blossoms, and individuals move fully into their wisdom phase. This cycle is linked to a sixth Jupiter return at age 72, and for most it is quite Jupiterian in nature. When it is not, Jupiter may permit escape from the body.

Fifth Demi-Return, 82.25 Years

The significant event of this hemi-cycle is the Uranus Return at age 84. Many choose to leave at this point, while others choose senile dementia as an escape from life. Meanwhile, the creative and wise who peaked at age 73 can enjoy the new lifestyle that is their reward for exploring new realms of experience. This event marks the beginning of a new evolutionary phase through which inspiration and invention flows freely for those who recognize its possibilities.

Sixth Return, 91.5 Years

Saturn makes its third return at age 88.5, while the fourth Saturn return confers galactic citizenship. This means that beginning at the midpoint of the fifth nodal cycle we become light bearers. From this point on we are not here to do; for our remaining years our presence is our gift to the world. Having overcome much, we are the living example of synchronicity between rising consciousness and continuity of life. We have become the Living Light and the Living Word, Ambassadors from the Spiritual Realm.

"Luck" at the North Node

By house, the North Node represents a lucky place. In that house certain resources are available quite consistently, and can be seen in hindsight.

First House: You will always be noticed. This can be an advantage in career or a disadvantage in a life of crime.

Second House: You will always have personal funds sufficient for your needs—as understood or according to beliefs.

Third House: You find or acquire the vehicle you wanted in unusual ways. People may give you a car or finance it for you.

Fourth House: Homes are readily available, and are sometimes provided in extraordinary ways.

Fifth House: You are a winner at gambling, and seem to know how to do this.

Sixth House: You can get the job you want, simply by deciding it's yours.

Seventh House: Your partner is noticed and you benefit from this.

Eighth House: Insurance pays off. You may be lucky about taxes. Some people inherit money, especially in the area of marital assets, and divorce settlements are advantageous.

Ninth House: There are travel opportunities and college scholarships, and writers can be lucky with editors.

Tenth House: Career opportunities come your way, along with high visibility. Some are famous.

Eleventh House: Friends and organizational contacts are lucky. You can make your own luck from hope or wishes reiterated, or with a group ritual.

Twelfth House: The pattern of luck or opportunity may be so random as to be hard to see. Even when unlucky in work or health, any losses in the sixth house turn out to be twelfth-house gains. With this placement, an avocation, institution, or mysterious source will be lucky. Much depends on the level of trust and what you trust in.

Part II

The Part of Fortune and the Astral Body

Part of Fortune/Pars Fortuna

Placed in charts almost as often as the lunar nodes is a circle containing a cross, either upright or positioned like an X. It is called the (Arabian) Part of Fortune, Fortuna or Pars Fortuna. As with the lunar nodes, I found information on it to be scarce and vague.

Fortuna is an abstract point calculated by adding the celestial longitudes of the Moon and Ascendant and subtracting the longitude of the Sun.[50] A more simple method is to create a chart with the Sun on the Ascendant, and then calculate how far the Sun was moved in the process. Add the same number of degrees to the placement of the Moon and you will have the placement of the Part of Fortune. The Part of Fortune is really a lunar Ascendant.

Certain meanings can be inferred from this information. Any Ascendant represents a form or structure created for a specific purpose that is derived from its point of origin/creator. It is an energy field. If we refer to our Sun as our purpose, the Ascendant is a structure formed specifically for the performance of that purpose. We may then conclude that Fortuna is a structure created for a lunar purpose. As the Ascendant describes our physical body and lifestyle, Pars Fortuna describes our astral/emotional body and lifestyle.

The Moon in the chart represents the emotional state of the mother during that period before and after birth when the child is not differentiated from the mother. It is more how she feels about herself than how she feels about the child, but the child absorbs these feelings as its own. They become the foundation for the emotional structure of the native. When learned behavior is shorted out by extreme stress or artificial mood alteration, the original feelings absorbed from the mother take over.

If we add the Sun/spirit and the Ascendant/form it takes and subtract/abstract the Lunar Mother effect, we have a point of *uncontaminated* or personal contact between them. This will represent

---

[50]When a chart is reversed, usually in the case of left-handed natives, Fortuna must be recalculated, using the new Ascendant (the original Descendant). It will be in the same degree as the original one, the same house and the opposite sign, in the new chart.

the feeling structure or astral body as it has developed during earlier phases and incarnations. If the Moon represents the Earth Mother, Pars Fortuna represents the Cosmic or Spiritual Mother. We might think of this point as our personal Goddess-Image, even as the Sun represents our God-Image. Sun is Spirit/Light Body.

When we view life as an electro-magnetic system, the Sun functions as a power plant, the Moon as a transformer, the Moon's nodes as personal wiring. The Ascendant is the *object of empowerment*—an engine, an appliance, a light, etc. We, the physical form of us described by the Ascendant, become an electrical field, a structure through which power/spirit acts.

The Moon has a great deal to do with needs, being the place from which the energy supply required to create physical form appears to originate. It describes the womb and the nest, from and into which we were born. In the beginning, we look to the Moon/mother/family for our needs, whether physical, emotional, or intellectual. This is where we are at home. Here we are fed, nurtured, disciplined—or not. It is usually where and from whom we learn to speak.

A physical-emotional bond is created that has much magnetic/attractive power. When we are over-nurtured or under-disciplined, it is difficult to relax that bond sufficiently to make the emotional move from childhood to adulthood. Until we achieve emotional adulthood, our nodal activity will be restricted and our Fortuna will be weak and anemic.

The means of empowering such a Part of Fortune is *in our own hands*. When we balance the Nodal Axis, our consciousness rises and we learn to structure our lives in ways that eliminate triggers to the weak areas of our emotional structure. The point is always to heal the present, not the past. This is a matter of energy dynamics. If the energy flows smoothly through our chart/life, life will gradually and effortlessly succeed.

In describing life as an electromagnetic system, we say that any physical form is a place where attention transforms the wave aspect of light to a particle aspect. These particles are magnetized into clumps and integrated into formal structures. As these structures acquire more matter, they become increasingly visible. We usually experience the visible as solid and tangible, but that is our choice. If we are to use this knowledge purposefully, the process must be conscious. With minimal attention, it functions minimally.

When electrical energy/power/consciousness is in motion, being directed to a task, it naturally creates a magnetic field around the channel though which it flows. That magnetic field can be called the Part of Fortune. It is a place where we attract things into our lives—different from creating them. Normally, I might *create* a book, but I would *attract* publishers and readers.

The requirement for this is some type of action. If we do not act/create, the magnetic field is weak and not very attractive. The Fortune involved is a by-product or side-effect of conscious living. That explains why Fortuna has been so poorly defined in the past.[51] It could not truly come into its own until humanity evolved into a knowledge/consciousness of its own energy dynamics.

[51]The best source is *Joy and the Part of Fortune* by Martin Schulman, published by Samuel Weiser Inc.

As awareness rises so does electromagnetic activity. The more energy/spirit we have running through our lives the greater the magnetic field becomes. A little more attention to our personal dynamics gets a little more energy flowing. Imbalanced attention produces an energy imbalance. Our system will clog up producing poverty, illness in body, or discomfort in our lives. Our *fortune* is withheld or delayed.

Sometimes misunderstanding the way life is intended to work causes shorts in the system. This can result in power which goes round and round without accomplishing positive results. These dysfunctional wiring systems produce addictions, channeling energy meant for construction into destructive purposes. Depending on the duration and severity of dysfunction, intervention from outside will be necessary. The medical community may need to re-solder some connections before the consciousness can be retrained through individual counseling and/or group support.

While the remainder of the chart will describe both the impersonal and personal intent of a life, the lunar nodes and Part of Fortune will describe the actual energy flows, leading to or away from creative activity. The rest of the chart will say what; the Node-Fortuna complex will say how. It describes our capacity for conscious direction and application of energy/attention. Its level of function must correspond to the developmental level of the personality. Individuation requires personal applications. Socialization requires social applications. With these completed, the final application is to the Greater Whole. Because of this, real understanding of the complex could only emerge with a rise in the general level of awareness.

The Part of Fortune describes a type of Uranian Luck Factor. Like anything Uranian, it refers to the sudden, unusual, or unexpected appearance of something which has actually been accumulating weak energy and compounding it. When it gathers enough force, it manifests—often when your attention had moved elsewhere. Doing this, it encourages us to follow our life intent or spiritual commitment, trusting that our personal needs will be met.

Unless the nodal activity is being directed by the being—as opposed to the ego program-Fortuna will be doing very little, and delineating it will be almost useless. Normally we begin transformation with the nodal axis. However, if we are in a hurry or want to bypass the usual channels and we are adaptable, we may choose to begin with the Part of Fortune. To affirm what this point represents will force the rest of the system to comply. There is some risk in this, especially for those who find sudden or dramatic changes difficult, but we present it because it is an available choice. It has the effect of Chakra-raising exercises, which can shock a system awake or burn out circuits. Until you have real knowledge of and belief in your ability to handle power, we do not advise such a method.

Fortuna as a Lunar Ascendant

Any Ascendant is part of an image structure. Although Fortuna is normally the only point shown on the chart, by implication it has a Descendant, a Midheaven and an IC[52] Remember that this is an outline of your personal feelings,[53] not those you inherited from your birth environment. It will depend on or emerge from the Moon, but will be yours alone. Fortuna exists both before and after this incarnation and must be remembered before it can be recognized by anyone. In the past it has not been recognized at all. More recently its recognition came late in life. Moving into the next age, it will become conscious at an earlier and earlier chronological age. This will result from understanding the interactive roles of feelings and thoughts in the growth of awareness.

The point opposite Fortuna will represent how significant others react to your aura. It can show you how this differs from your real feelings. It can show how or why you attract the personal relationships that you do. A creative way to change this is to change the definition of the sign involved.

Examples: Capricorn: Change old to mature. Aries: change selfish to centered in the self. Libra: Change adversary to equal. Cancer: Change childish to growing.[54]

The point in waxing square (lunar IC) represents a private emotional structure. It describes how you interpret your feelings when you are alone or at home or what feelings predominate your quiet/private times. The point in waning square (lunar Midheaven) represents a public one. It describes how you feel in a public position. For deep self-awareness, regard this as emotional origins and goals.

Example: Cancer Fortuna will have Libra at the fourth, showing shared feelings. The Aries tenth shows that self realization can be experienced in a public way, successfully, and late in life.

---

[52]Use the degree of Fortuna and project it in an equilateral cross so that each point is square its neighbors. Advanced students who have a good computer astrology program may find it interesting to rectify the natal chart, placing the degree of Fortuna at the Ascendant.

[53]When any part of this cross falls in an interception, no part will fully activate until the interception is cleared. This is usually at a time chosen pre-incarnationally, and is most often shown by the transit of one or more outer planets across at least one side of the interception.

[54]First align your vision of Fortuna with the most positive side of house and sign.

Understand Fortuna as how you feel about life, and its opposing point as responses of significant others to your feelings. This can show a range of responses based on your expression of your true feelings. Remember that this cross cannot activate until adulthood, and its activity is usually not objectively observable before midlife. The emotional body is constructed from the experience of living with our feelings, of learning to express or deny them. Undirected feelings, unexpressed longings, and unclaimed intuitions go into it. When it accumulates enough substance to reach visibility, it can create a supply for our spiritual needs, even as the Moon attracts the substance to satisfy our physical/psychological needs.

Fortuna as Our Astral Body

Esoteric texts describe an astral body that interpenetrates the physical one. It is said to be comprised of energies in a slightly different electrical phase from the physical body. The astral body ranges from translucent to transparent, depending on the variation. It is visible to those with wide visual ranges as an aura.

Like the physical body it functions as a vehicle for consciousness. While the physical body is used to navigate physical reality, the astral body is the structure we use for Out-of-Body travel. Functioning as a Dreaming Body, its action is primarily spontaneous and instinctive. The exception to this, is the Conscious Dreamer.

As we said, Fortuna is a structure created for a lunar purpose. By sign and house, it describes our emotional body and lifestyle. Its popular name is Astral Body or Soul Body. Esoteric writers have called it a desire body because much of its substance is comprised of unfulfilled desires. There are truth and error in this.

Because of the need for human consciousness to evolve, the true origin of desire remained unknown until quite recently. It can be recognized by examining the word DE-SIRE. It means quite simply, "of the Father." Equally it means "of the Stars," with its origin in our Destiny or Spiritual Goal. In humankind, desire is an expression of the needs of Spirit.

In the natal chart, the Moon, as the mind of the body/feelings, represents physical needs and the source from which they originally come: mother.[55] If/when we mature sufficiently to individuate, we no longer expect mother/parents/family to satisfy those needs. The fully emancipated adult looks to self, society, or deity for that supply. Fortuna will describe that supply as an aspect or result of the level of nodal function, This must be assessed before delineating Fortuna.

As we achieve spiritual maturity/higher consciousness, we discover and begin our spiritual intent. This is synthesized from the entire chart. Begin with the Sun's description of the type of energy and personal purpose. Look at the nodal axis to discover where/how you can attract attention and

---

[55]Including Mother Earth.

where you naturally[56] project energy/attention. Pay particular attention to aspects to the nodal axis. Negative aspects to the nodes show that some type of struggle for appropriate attention overshadowed childhood. As a result, some type of life adjustment must be made in the interests of surviving to adulthood. That adjustment will haunt the adult life until an emotional transformation occurs. The emotional debris of this haunting becomes the substance of the astral body. A great deal of suppressed bitterness, grief, pain or anger can make the aura look muddy and dark. If/when/as greater self-realization changes the way we feel about the past, it will grow lighter and brighter. The brighter and clearer it becomes, the more attractive it will be. As it lightens, it attracts increasingly beneficial substance or experience into our lives.

---

[56]Anything naturally easy and successful originates in Sprit. Anything at struggle originates in your Ego Programming.

Pars Fortuna as the Astral Body

Fortuna's sign placement describes the type of emotional debris the astral body contains. A full range of possibilities described by that sign are available for attraction into life. The quality of its benefits is a direct outcome of the balance or imbalance of the nodal axis. Remember that it is the visible part of a four-point cross of emotional identity. Also look to the Moon to see what type of emotional foundation underlies the Astral Structure.

Aries Fortuna/Astral Body

Aries Fortuna describes emotional innocence and lack of experience. The native has probably not incarnated on earth recently. She or he is not as solid and impervious to emotional stress as others and can easily be hurt and/or frightened. Any invasion of the child's boundaries, whether physical or mental, may trigger its survival instincts. The astral body substance is fear, anger, frustration, and/or grief. It can hover around the native as a cloud of free-floating anxiety.

However, because Aries energy is raw and primitive it is amazingly malleable and will create whatever defenses are needed for the survival of body and/or personality. It needs to survive at all costs. The power of rage can be its most potent defensive weapon.

Its greatest asset is its innocence. Normally it does not see much of the negativity that surrounds it. When it is hurt or angry, the emotions are powerful but short-lived. Literally it uses a burst of energy to remove the threat, then goes on as though nothing had happened. Because it does not expect to be hurt, it does not create more negativity. Only when severe and/or repeated emotional or physical blows create paranoia, is there a severe problem.

The range of expression is from sociopath to young god/goddess. The place on that range can be assessed by weighing the innate strengths of the natal chart against the difficulties in the ego program. Always it is necessary to find a balance between personal innocence and social awareness. More than that, the emotional dependency of childhood must be moderated by achieving a balance between responsiveness to others and personal responsibility.

Clearing the aura will be a matter of understanding that the suffering incurred is impersonal, a product of being a child in a world of adults who are still emotional children. If the native can run over all the obstacles—and usually she or he can—the aura will achieve increasing clarity as the years go by. It is common for the Aries astral body to resemble that of a child—clear and innocent, full of energetic expectation—even at an advanced age.

Taurus Fortuna/Astral Body

Taurus Fortuna describes emotional tenacity or possessiveness, especially of the body. This native may not have been off the earth recently. She or he is amazingly solid, with the feelings and emotions keyed entirely to the maintenance of physical structure. Any violation of the body or the value system will trigger withdrawal. The astral body is often more solid and visible than the physical one and traumatized natives hide within or behind it. This permits the projection of an image that is larger and/or more powerful than their actual size and strength. Much obesity is directly traceable to this factor.

Taurus Fortuna's greatest asset is its personal magnetism. It attracts a great deal of experience, integrating positive and negative in ways that illustrate the ways good overcomes evil. Although sometimes a crisis personality, the inherent love in Taurus always overcomes the hatred of Scorpio adversaries. Individuals can find a neutral position at the center where they can stand on the foundation of Leo spiritual heritage, realizing a goal of passing on that heritage to the (Aquarius) future. At some levels of awareness this can permit the accumulation of a considerable estate provided there is an impersonal or transpersonal goal for doing so.

The range of expression is from poverty hiding behind a large image to wealth surrounding a clear image, optimally designed for carrying out the spiritual imperative. Always it is necessary to integrate desire into the need system so that sufficient substance[57] can be acquired to show others the absolute creative power of impersonal love.

Clearing the aura and reducing the physical body will be a matter of realizing inherent self-worth. The merging of desire and need generates great power. With power reclaimed, we may safely claim our inheritance, allowing it to pass through our lives on its path to the future. This transforms dense matter to clear energy. The astral body then clears revealing the true physical dimensions. The appearance is one of draining a large accumulation of fluid from the body, permitting it to return to normal size.

Gemini Fortuna/Astral Body

Gemini Fortuna describes two (usually overlapping) astral bodies, like conjoined twins. This image shows a bonding difficulty and usually has a different expression for males and females. It literally describes half-bonding or dual bonding. In the first case the initial nurturer is the only person close enough to the child to create a bond. Sometimes the mother is very possessive and does not allow

---

[57]Money, housing, transportation, etc.

anyone else to touch the baby. Occasionally, the mother and child

are alone and isolated. At the appropriate time for separation, no father is physically or emotionally present to help the process.

If the Self is reasonably strong/evolved, the child will find ways to separate sufficiently to be able to feel some of its own feelings, but will find the mother's feelings invading consciousness on a regular basis. Effectively, mixed feelings occur in some part of the psyche. The greater her hold, the greater the resulting confusion over what the native feels. In some cases this is the sole cause of difficulties in sexual identity. This can *look like* bisexuality. If you have these feelings and they are not a problem, simply accept it. If you have them and they are a problem, you will need to use some techniques to rid yourself of the possession. Usually this is a male issue because his feelings are divided between his own *male needs* and his mother's *female needs*. Question what you feel, especially if it does not appear entirely rational or compatible with other parts of your life. The simple recognition that some of your feelings may not be your own will begin to resolve the problem. Gradually the two astral bodies will merge into one, which is the product or *offspring* of the two.

The more common female version of a double astral body comes from being emotionally possessed by Mother and physically possessed by Father or some other male. Here the child's need for separation from Mother is so great that it is drawn into a second incestuous bond. In this case, the native's own feelings tend to disappear entirely. This can be so painful as to require the anesthesia of an addiction for survival.

These women, quite literally, cannot feel their own feelings. This allows them to be overwhelmed by the feelings of others nearby. They can be so psychically open to the slightest negativity as to have their life filled with *allergic reactions* to substances and persons. Substance reactions always have their real origins in emotional contamination. The half-bonded person will experience some of this. The double-bonded one will have increasingly severe reactions over a lifetime unless or until the core issue is addressed. Many learn to use alcohol or drugs to numb their feeling receptors and/or to dull the pain. Most have work and/or sex addictions. For the vast majority, healing can only come when control of their lives is given to some higher power. Usually this means an ongoing involvement in some *Anonymous* program.

The range of experience is from multiple personality disorder to trance channels. Much will depend on the range of awareness available and a belief system that allows you to explore your own consciousness.

Your greatest asset is your rationality. You notice that some feelings do not make sense. Clearing the aura will be a matter of removing the influence of one or both parental figures. This will allow you to function from your own feelings. Effectively this equals a second birth. At that time, it will be critical to be surrounded with people of positive feelings, so that any new bonding will serve your purposes. This is usually called creating a family of choice. When this is successful, the duality of Gemini will simply refer to an emotional structure that was one thing in the past and another in the present. Effectively, one astral body will move behind, or be absorbed into, the other. You can assist the formation and maintenance of this unity by naming the astral body perfect, whole, and complete, fully matured and fully mastered.

The experience will feel like your emotions are receding into the background of your life where they no longer run it. As the feeling structure clears of parental influence, you will feel immensely freer than you have ever felt. Your mind will be clearer than it has ever been. In the end, you get a personally conscious astral body, awake and aware of your true purpose in life.

Cancer Fortuna/Astral Body

Cancer Fortuna describes emotional birth, growth, and/or rebirth. The initial astral body is small, even fetal. It remains inside the physical body for many years for protection. A Moon-ruled Fortuna has difficulty separating from the original feelings of the mother. Until that occurs, mother and her feelings condition the identity. Natives tend to live their lives satisfying what are really her emotional needs. It appears that the mother projects her own karma onto her child through the Cancer Fortuna.

Cancer's greatest asset is a capacity for continuing and rapid growth. It will continue to grow within whatever boundaries surround it, until it literally outgrows them and is projected out.[58] In many cases, these individuals cannot fully individuate until the birth mother dies. The exceptions are those who are able to divorce themselves from her. Even so, some type of help is needed. A ritual dedicated to releasing mother and cutting the mother-child bond can be helpful. If you can get past the programming it often violates, prayers/requests for assistance can be directed to saints, god/goddesses, other discarnate helpers, or directly to deity.

Exception to the usual rule: The technique of setting a boundary/circle taught elsewhere usually does not work because the inhibitor is inside our psyche. Sometimes we mistake it for a kind of pregnancy, so that it brings up subliminal abortion issues. Most significant of all, is the fact that this Fortuna usually belongs to an evolved being. It is impossible for others to survive the kind of birth issue it contains. An evolved being is a loving being. The necessary psychic surgery to remove this type of mother-possession seems to be cruel. Cruelty is impossible to such a one. From this comes the need to get assistance in the process.

When natives have long-lived mothers, her need to control us often runs our lives for years. Finally, release comes and we are reborn, with our own needs running our creative processes. Like any rebirth process, there will be an initial pregnancy and labor process. Releasing any fetus requires

---

[58]A native with this placement, well into her forties, had this flashback: I was out of body, watching my mother give birth to me. She was lying in the bed with body completely rigid and fists clenched. The doctor spoke with authority, calling her name. He ordered her, "Stop that!" The shock of being spoken to in that tone caused her to release the body tension. Instantly, I was back in that tiny body, clawing my way out of my mother. he native adds: "I have been *clawing my way out of* one situation after another for most of my adult life."

some stretching of our physical boundaries and the use of some normally unused muscles. There is pain involved in this, but the pain disappears with remarkable speed once the rebirth is complete. After that our lives begin to work smoothly and easily, moving toward the true intention and goal of life. This is a growth process and does not result in overnight success, but the growth is rapid and can reach maturity in a few years. In the meantime we can expect our true Source to provide for us, those things that support our growing awareness.

Expression ranges from an inability to leave home to the ability to leave home forever at an early age. Most fall somewhere between, with lives that are focused on getting, having, or keeping certain security blankets that have more to do with mother's life than our own. Spiritual seekers who have difficulty realizing that these things are not personal needs will have them removed in a transformation process. For some period of time (nine months is classic) natives will live without these things always recognized as needs.

Clearing the aura will result as natives distance themselves from their mothers, but full freedom from her can only come as a rebirth process. After that the sustaining flow of life runs smoothly and Fortuna brings real joy.

Leo Fortuna/Astral Body

Leo Fortuna describes emotional drama as an activating force for the adult need system. These individuals have an inherent need to claim their spiritual inheritance. They are the lost princes/princesses of life, growing up in the homes of spiritual peasants. Usually the mother/family believes in the sanctity of poverty, or that their role in life is to suffer patiently. Such families take pride in living humbly, as though such lives grant extra points toward the heavenly prize. Meanwhile, the resources denied hinder the development of inborn talents. When those talents manifest spontaneously, the ego program dictates the life of a starving artist on the premise that starvation improves talent. This is, of course, completely irrational. Raising awareness through the nodal axis will reveal the deception and the sin[59] of excessive humility.

Leo Fortuna's greatest asset is its spiritual heritage. As a direct heir to Deity, creative abilities are close to the surface of consciousness. Developing the nodal axis will bring protection, permitting innate talents to develop. Implicit in the Leo Fortuna is the possibility of hearing a Divine Voice say, "This is my beloved child, in whom I am well pleased."

The range of expression will be from the great pretender to the world-acclaimed artist. The place on that range can be assessed by synthesizing the signs of the Sun, the Ascendant, and the fifth house. This will show who really owns the chart, along with how she or he is supposed to look and act. Add the North Node to see what gets attention and the South Node to see where it can be passed on. Negative aspects to these areas slow or limit the process, dimming the Leo light. Even so, darkness never overwhelms the light and the talent will never be destroyed. At worst it will hide behind the facade of the Ascendant. At best it will enlighten the native's personal world.

[59]Literally: error/missing the center of the target.

The aura will clear spontaneously as natives achieve greater self-realization. Knowing who/what we are, what our true heritage is, shows us the evolutionary level from which we are born. This frees us to truly express our spiritual heritage through our role in life. We then live in the world, as the light of the world. We might equally say that we give it color and beauty.

Virgo Fortuna/Astral Body

Virgo Fortuna describes emotional purity. At this point the emotional structure is fully formed as a clear stream of consciousness. Because this potentiality has gone unrecognized in the general consciousness, historically these natives have experienced emotions as painful. Allowing themselves to feel fortunate has triggered guilt in the ego structure. Here the belief in crucified Christs and suffering saints has been most destructive. Whenever these began to function easily, from spiritual energy, they believed that they were in violation of some moral code. Feeling good triggered ego judgment, reversing the flow and causing them to feel bad. The only rational solution to such a dilemma is numbing the feeling structure to unconsciousness. Still, the need to become conscious of Fortuna keeps it bouncing from one pole to the other.

Its greatest asset is the clarity of reason. Eventually natives notice that what they are feeling does not make sense. By analyzing the need system and weighing it against the family belief system, the truth can be revealed and trust in the natural instincts can become trust in the intuitive function.[60]

The range of expression is from slaves to paid professionals. In the former, their own love has been used against them. The only power that truly holds them is their own, projected into the hands of another. They may notice an unusual ability to endure punishment and think it obligates them to be victims. It does not. These must learn to reclaim their power, to claim their rights, and/or to administer some tough love. Most Virgo Fortunas spend time in co-dependent relationships. When they can realize that this is no more loving that letting a small child eat nothing but candy, they will be on their way to freedom.

The end stage is that of the well-paid professional. Most will be in serving professions. They will be healers, teachers, counselors[61], etc. After that, recognition and welcome can greet the personal feeling structure. When it does, the astral body will resemble a clear, cool, stream from which we can drink. As the astral body clears, the Spiritual body begins to be visible behind it. This equals being able to see our spiritual path clearly. That path will take on the aspects of a flowing river, and we can let it carry us back to the Divine Sea of Spirit.

Libra Fortuna/Astral Body

Libra Fortuna describes an emotional loss of innocence. Natives have recently spent much time on earth. Too much experience has overwhelmed innocence. The astral body contains substance of

---

[60]These are, quite literally, the same thing. Those things we do instinctively, without thought, emerge from the intuitive portion of our mental structure.

[61]These are very broad categories, intended to include astrologers, reiki masters, metaphysicians, etc.

unmade choices and conflicting judgments. It can look like a mask, light on one side, dark on the other. Literally, energy is almost equally divided between spiritual intention and ego instruction so that the demands of society pull these natives off track. Whatever they do, the inner voice or an outer one objects. Sometimes the only choice seems to be between two evils and life can be too much. Survival of the spiritual identity is the absolute imperative. If necessary, natives will withdraw from a body/ego/Ascendant too heavy and burdened to carry.

Its greatest asset is its ability to weigh alternatives on a fine scale, selecting the better of two nearly equal choices. Here we may learn that there are negative aspects to any choice. Alternatively, we discover that everything is good for something. Libra Fortuna, as an astral body, is the gate to the future. If we turn back, we return to Aries and continue on the karmic wheel. If we walk through the gate, we must learn to survive in society. During our social journey we will experience much growth in consciousness, learning to rightly divide the word of truth[62].

The range of expression depends on choosing to live or die for Deity. Natives are forever confronted with the consensus beliefs of the local society. They may lapse into childish acceptance of them, make peace with them, or begin to create lives independent of them. The first choice becomes an end in itself. A second avoids the choice by numbing the mind, giving away choice to others. A third will lead to an understanding of the purpose of ego as a structure for learning about the world. It offers the opportunity to marry ego and identity, learning to live in inner harmony and outer peace.

When inner harmony is achieved, the aura will clear as a sign that the inner marriage has been achieved. At this point the dual nature as mammal and deity are consciously united, joining hands and hearts in dedication to the spiritual path and commitment to the conscious way.

Scorpio Fortuna/Astral Body

Scorpio Fortuna describes emotional intensity or passion. The astral body will resemble a white hole or a black hole. It is the womb of rebirth. Always it implies transformation of energy to form or form to energy. In each case something dies so that something else may live. The astral body is literally composed of our feelings about life and death. Few are neutral on either subject. The volume of feelings crammed into the emotional body requires them to be compacted, making it very light or very dark, filled with hope or with despair. This can be projected as a love of life. Included will be acceptance of its changing forms. Alternatively, it can be projected as hatred of life fused with fear of death.

Its greatest asset is its passion. Passion is power. Power creates, destroys, and recreates the structures of life. Sometimes Scorpio burns itself up in ardor, but doing so, like a Phoenix, it rises again. In the process it is offered the opportunity to take control of its own transformative process through merging ego and identity into a unit. The entire being structure becomes a Soul—a channel—for

---

[62]Bible, New Testament, II Timothy 2:15.

creative energies to be transferred from one reality to another. They can make things visible disappear. They can make things invisible appear. Theirs is a mastery over the conversion of energy to matter, to energy, to matter to. . . . More accurately, they have discovered how to raise and lower vibrations in living structures.

These beings have great personal magnetism and the range of expression runs from a sex addict to a Merlin. They can infuse life in a dying body whose task is incomplete, or drain energy from an ego compulsion, allowing it to die. The power is used to destroy the obsolete and to quicken the seeds of new creation.

Theirs is a mission, whether it looks creative or destructive. Someone has to weed the garden of life and someone has to replant the annual crops. These auras are only seen through the eyes of our ego judgments. If they are aligned with the divine purpose, even the darkest of these will be experienced as potentiality. When the owners of such astral bodies understand the creative potential of destructive force, good overcomes evil and light overcomes darkness. This is the realization that turns up the light to an intensity so bright it disappears from the ordinary visual range. Scorpio Fortuna is hard to see, being too dark or too bright for human eyes!

Sagittarius Fortuna/Astral Body

Sagittarius Fortuna may seem to be a rainbow mantle or a shifting, sparkling, stellium of stars. Having emerged from Scorpio's dark night of the soul, she or he finds the glorious promise of sunshine after a storm. The intensity has cleared, spread out, and become a canopy of light and color. It describes emotional variety and the wisdom to delight in its experience without becoming caught in the physical senses. These natives can slip their consciousness in and out of form at will. This astral body is a traveler of the world, the universe, the totality.

Here the meaning of relationship is made manifest. The internalized alchemist is now the Wise One or Magi, able to apply alchemy as information processing. Being an expert on language, this Fortuna is fully aware of the implications of IN-FORM-ATION, able to use it for the increase of consciousness on all levels. The multiplicity of Sagittarius applies to a broad range of awareness.

Scorpio's fusion principle now takes another step. In the beginning, Love and Light divided to produce formal structures and a consciousness capable of seeing, naming, learning about them. Structural judgments are lost in Scorpio. Sagittarius merges consciousness with purified love.[63] Principles and symbols link so that the Sagittarian Sage can think and work with either or both in simultaneous time.

Their ability for astral travel is so refined that if they find, upon incarnation in a body, that circumstances will severely restrict its work, it will simply withdraw. For this reason we never see cloudiness in the Sagittarian astral body. To senses still functioning within a physical range it is probably the most beautiful one around. Some call these the faerie people!

---

[63]Acceptance, approval.

Capricorn Fortuna/Astral Body

Capricorn Fortuna stands at the gate between this world and the next. She or he turns, looks back, and reviews the climb. It is like achieving the mountaintop, then pausing for breath. A decision must be made about whether to go back the way we came or on down the other side. This is a fail-safe point, where we must choose to go on or go back. Either way we move, the decision will be final[64]. It can feel like being caught between two worlds, at home in neither.

The astral body will contain the substance of all the remaining ego boundaries. It can be as dark and impenetrable as Sagittarius was bright and beautiful because it represents stalled energy. Anything Sagittarius put off until tomorrow must be dealt with in Capricorn. The longer it stalls the more solid it gets. The longer you look at Capricorn's boundaries the more difficult it becomes to resume motion. Many Capricorns lose mobility or consciousness by default. Refusal to make a decision becomes a decision, committing Being to return to the karmic wheel.

Capricorn is the sign of full human maturity. It bridges the end of being social humanity and the beginning of divine humanity. The choice and the responsibility for making it is ours. To the outer senses the gate may seem to be locked or blocked by things we perceive as having been left undone. The inner senses know that evolution does not depend on physical activity. It is the product of self-awareness. The self-aware being knows that some things are learned best by doing, but others can be learned from the experience of others. Seen this way, we know that there is nothing left undone. We may give ourselves permission to leave incarnate life, and/or the wheel of karma. The only locks or bars on the gate are the ones we have projected there. These are not real, but only thought forms. At this point we may literally walk through the gate—without opening it!

Expression ranges from a dark brooding density to a light so white as to be transparent. It contains the full range of human possibilities and all the available choices. Natives can go directly to the next level at the end of childhood or they can be still pounding on the gate with bloody fists or head at advanced ages. The tenacity of earth keeps them determined to win and that determination can keep them alive in bodies that should long ago have died. It was for these that Richard Bach wrote the book *Illusions*. In it the hero learns to walk on water and swim in the earth.

Sitting on the mountaintop will make your body or your life rigid and increasingly difficult to move. But moving into the next dimension does not require a physical structure. It is simply a matter of shifting your consciousness, your awareness. By the time we reach Capricorn Fortuna, the astral body is tied to the physical only by personal will. That much authority over life can only come from a powerfully creative consciousness. You may then choose to reformulate your body or to leave it behind. Literally, when the astral body is cleared it is healed. It can then take the place of the physical one and walk the earth like an angelic being, with a heavenly body. This is the reality behind those Yogi Masters who are no longer subject to the demands of a physical body. Alternatively, you can leave this reality entirely. It is your right and your choice.

---

[64]From our point of view.

Aquarius Fortuna/Astral Body

Aquarius Fortuna is comprised of the knowledge gleaned from the entire previous cycle of spiritual development. Aquarius is the freest sign in the zodiac, living between two realities with consciousness of and access to both. This is the truly objective being, able to see an extended reality with clarity and truth. In it there is no judgment. Its perspective is so far out that unconsciousness and consciousness can be seen as two interactive sides of reality.

Astral bodies of the first ten signs all interpenetrate the physical body. At Aquarius it has begun to separate and looks like a globe or oval of light above and/or partly behind the physical body. It has been mistaken for a high chakra, floating over the head. Primarily white light, it may have a faint tint of color from the Sun sign, showing intention.

Its greatest asset is non-attachment. It understands the value of everything and condemns nothing. Because of this it is free to move into and out of world consciousness. Its function is like that of the bees that pollinate so much of the plant world. Without them, world consciousness might not flower and reproduce. The evolutionary process might stop. Literally, their function is to act as channels between the layers of reality. They are the creators, the inventors, the inspiration or activation of new possibilities in human consciousness. These are the guardians who watch over the evolution of the general consciousness. They can project an image that seems as solid and real as any human but is the most magnificent illusion of life. These are the spiritual adepts, able to appear and disappear at will. Yet they know the human experience well enough to avoid doing anything too far outside the experience of those whose lives they touch. It is not their intent to frighten, coerce, or overwhelm their more substantial friends on earth.

The form taken is often that of the creative genius or child prodigy. It is as though their child bodies cannot entirely contain the magnitude of knowledge and experience represented by Fortuna. The astral body hangs over them, using that body to channel extraordinary talent into the visible world.

Pisces Fortuna/Astral Body

Pisces Fortuna describes unstructured essence. The physical form is seen through a film of translucent awareness. With this placement, Spirit, Soul, and Body blend into an undivided whole and it is impossible to separate the physical body from the astral and spiritual bodies.

Our human journey is from the birth of individuality to the birth of unity to the rebirth of individuality. It takes us into form, makes the form conscious, then consciously dissolves the form into the identity structure. In Pisces, the formal structure is almost dissolved, leaving only a ghost of form. Here the sense of identity functions as a solid shape. There is no question of self-image; there may be a question of self. The reality is that the two are merged into a single structure, more energy than matter. When this happens, Soul is also absorbed or disappears within the structure simply because, with no space between them, no passageway between spirit and body is necessary. The only real channel will then be Fortuna. It will bridge Heaven and Earth as a Channel of Blessing to many.

With Pisces Fortuna, what you see is what you get. This is the totally honest being, completely true to a self fully identified with Source. It is said that during pregnancy and early infancy a child does not know that it is not part of its mother. This is the spiritual equivalent of that, when there is no differentiation between the gestating seeds of the next phase[65] and the form that contains it in this one.

Consciousness has merged, once more, with the substance of reality. This being is a developing idea in the mind of god/goddess. It is the seed of a new creation, functioning in the last vestiges of a dissolving form. It has no real boundaries of its own. Its essence fills whatever space is created for it. If it seems willful, it is because the Divine will expresses directly through it. Divinity, being perfect, whole, and complete knows itself to be absolutely right and good. There are no exceptions, no dilutions. From the idea to the manifestation is but a heartbeat.

Because of this, many resent these beings. The master Jesus spoke of it in Matthew 10:16-42. Verse 37 is quite explicit about where loyalty must lie. We recommend that anyone with the Pisces Fortuna read the entire passage, which names both the difficulties and the rewards of the apostle. That is the true designation for the Pisces astral body.

Natives must recognize their apostleship and the value of it. They must give up all attempts at compliance with the shoulds in consensus reality. Compliance cramps the feeling structure and this one is entirely too powerful and too oriented to species survival to risk harming it. Here we have a child (at one level) with the powers of a Merlin. It ill behooves anyone to harm this child. As adults these natives assume guardianship of this inner child. No person or circumstance must be permitted to harm it. It is critical to respond to your feelings because they are keyed to the survival of the future of humanity. Do not permit any part of your life to be abused. Neither indulge in so much pride as to prevent your asking your true parents[66] for assistance. You may have anything you ask for[67].

---

[65]The best definition of *phase* given us is: The personal equivalent of an Astrological Age. Traditional esoteric texts would call it moving to another hierarchy.

[66]Father God, Mother Earth. The human ones are, in parental terms, illusions—not your parents at all.

[67]. . . *in my name*. In my nature—by going within to the god-consciousness.

Using the Part of Fortune in the Signs

When the energy system is working smoothly and the spiritual goals are being accomplished, the Part of Fortune will describe, by sign, the aspect of being which will be activated as a magnetic field. Remember to keep all delineations positive so that this point really describes the joyous feeling of being fortunate in attracting those things which make us feel happy and personally fulfilled. Notice the elements here. Fire brings spiritual rewards in terms of joy and enthusiasm, which are naturally attractive. Air brings rewards in terms of mental activity, which can always be turned to a profit. Water brings emotional rewards, which means the fulfillment of all needs and desires. Earth brings tangible rewards; prosperity usually arrives by a direct route.

Aries Part of Fortune

Aries Fortuna describes the outcome of balancing the nodes as self-realization. It is the discovery of our rightful *name*, heritage, and identity. As consciousness rises, we begin to notice and change the ways in which we use the phrase, "I am. . . ." It is imperative that we learn to notice what we are calling ourselves. If we call the self a pig, it can only expect to receive garbage for food and a wallow for its home. This placement shows us how powerful human consciousness is and that it can override the spiritual reality. Kidnap the heir to a throne at birth and rear it in the home of a peasant and it will believe that it is a peasant. She or he will create or attract only such things are appropriate for a peasant. The most productive use of this Fortuna is to rename the self as the true offspring and heir of the Original I AM, to claim the name and fame of god/goddess. With that naming and claiming a very high powered magnetic field is generated and *ANYTHING* is possible.

Financial Affirmation: I am wealthy, or I am the owner of_____.

Taurus Part of Fortune

Taurus Fortuna describes the outcome of balancing the nodes as self-worth. It means that we can have whatever, and as much as we believe that we deserve. The more positive regard we have for self; the greater the rewards. It will be critical with this placement to understand that these rewards are for the self first and that all giving must be from the excess. Our universe will not give you your needs and desires if you are not willing to keep what is designated yours. This means that you are not permitted to sacrifice your life to those whose only claim is that they need you. You will be required to release *the need to be needed*. These funds are designated for the Nodal Purpose. The Christian Bible commands that we not cast our pearls before swine. That command applies directly to Taurus Part of Fortune.

Financial Affirmation: I am worth a million dollars (or any other figure you choose).

Gemini Part of Fortune

Gemini Part of Fortune describes the outcome of balancing the nodes as dual, allowing us multiple magnetic fields—question, need, desire.[68] Each creates a vacuum of its own type that attracts the appropriate response. Each can express in its own area, in parallel, or in series. In parallel applications the questions and the needs are separate expressions so that the appearance is of having two magnetic fields. One will answer questions; the other supplies physical needs. This can be either more or less evolved/conscious than the series process.

The series process generates a question like, "Where can I find what I want/need or how can I get . . . ?" Here cause and effect are used consciously and with intent. This method involves the intentional use of mental cause to achieve objective effect. Neither is better than the other; the choice is yours.

Financial Affirmation: I need/want $5,000; where is it? This defines or names the magnetic field as one of need and question, both of which are attractive. The money may arrive in form or it may arrive in the form of a marketable idea. It is important to keep open to all possibilities with this placement.

Cancer Part of Fortune

Cancer Part of Fortune describes the outcome of balancing the nodes as a growth or growing magnetic field, a place where something can be gestated. It is literally about getting in touch with our own real needs. Cancer Part of Fortune is particularly effective for the Aquarian method of energy layering. Depending on the overall level of consciousness, it may represent a growth in quantity or in quality.

Practically, it refers to the need to depend on Source to give us our needs, from the understanding that as we take on greater responsibilities in the world, our needs will be met with increasing ease and plenty. The purer and clearer our feeling function the more aware of our real needs we become. This results in a more consistent ability to make space in our lives for the arrival of those things which are truly needed for our purpose.

_____
[68]Remember that a desire is merely a need of the spirit.

This placement has the potential to grow into a realization that if I feel the need of it, if I want it, I am expressing a need/desire of the mother spirit which is gestating me. This makes supply automatic. It allows living with *no visible means of support*. Our finances have no direct connection to our work, but are direct expressions of nurture by Source.

Financial Affirmation: I need this bill paid; I want a new car. Acknowledge the feeling involved, for it is the feeling and the intensity with which it is felt that creates the void for the universe to fill. *Feel the empty space* that has been defined by your statement.

Leo Part of Fortune

Leo Part of Fortune describes the outcome of balancing the nodes as an inherited talent. It requires us to praise our gifts, and be thankful for them. Too much humility is out of place and a hindrance. Literally, Leo confers royalty, so we must begin to state our requests in the context of mentioning what we want to our royal parent, in the knowledge and expectation that the parent can and will give us what we want or need the moment that she or he becomes aware that we want or need it. The Leo Part of Fortune magnetic field attracts at the level of inheritance we claim. We can think of self as the heir of a family, a clan, a county, state, or nation. Our heritage is as great as we are willing to claim, and what we attract in life will correspond with our claim.

This placement has the potential for realization that, "It is the Father's good pleasure to give us all that we ask or need."

Financial Affirmation: Dad, can I have the Cadillac today? Mother, can I wear your green dress to the party? I want part of my (unlimited) trust fund for a trip to Europe. Always these requests come from a place of expectation that they will be granted because you are the beloved heir of the most wealthy parents around.

Virgo Part of Fortune

Virgo Part of Fortune describes the outcome of balancing the nodes as one of function. Here resources can be taken for granted and requests are about using them to do something which we want or need to do. Since the magnetic field is perfected, needing only practice, these requests, like the Leo ones, should be made in expectation of a yes answer. You are simply informing-notice that this word implies putting something into form—the parent spirit of your desire, need, or intention to do something, in the full expectation that the resources for doing it are readily available. Jesus of Nazareth said, "*The things I do, ye shall do, and greater things.*" This Part of Fortune is destined to make us conscious of unlimited choice.

Financial Information: I want to drive the Porsche to work today. I need to wear the tuxedo to the company party. The preexisting condition is that we must be doing *spiritual work*. Full realization means that anything we do is spiritual work. Wherever Virgo is, consciousness is the key. In whatever way we categorize our activity, we will be supplied accordingly. The volume of supply will be directly related to the importance we attach to what we are doing.

Libra Part of Fortune

Libra Part of Fortune describes the outcome of balancing the nodes as one of relation. Here we claim our connection with Source and expect to share the assets of the partnership. This placement gives us a *joint bank account* with Source. We must claim our adult status and become partners in the spiritual plan for earth. Having done so, we are entitled to all the rights and privileges of full partnership in the *family business* or the *grand design*. What is received seems to be a gift because it is an external expression, not an internal one. Up to Libra, it is possible to earn or create. From Libra on, we must accept our fortune as something which is drawn from our treasures laid up in heaven.

Financial Affirmation: At this point it is no longer necessary to specify forms or amounts. The request must be for my share. I want/need my share of the profits for 1995, or my *company residence or company car*, etc. While this can be limited by a too-small view of the share we are entitled to, what is received tends always to be a bit more than what we expected and, over time, this has a cumulative effect.

Caution: No judgment on what is received is allowed. Accept what you get with thankfulness. If it looks strange, ask what it is good for. Never declare anything which comes to you "no-good"; never refuse the gift. All has a purpose and each purpose leads to a greater share of the profits.

Scorpio Part of Fortune

Scorpio Part of Fortune describes the outcome of balancing the nodes as an inheritance or an investment that pays interest and/or dividends. Very often this is the form in which our luck is received. At this point the personal assets begin to pay off as the fusion of *mine*/Taurus and *yours*/Scorpio becomes ours. This allows us direct access to all that is, giving us the power to command the very essence of life to conform to our needs and desires. This is the placement of the magician/sorcerer.

Financial Affirmation: With this placement an affirmation is almost unnecessary. As soon as the native notices a need or desire it begins to manifest its own fulfillment. It is as though cause and effect have merged. All that is required is that the need or desire be noticed, perhaps mentioned. If the energy flow is poor, there may be a need to repeat the attention, but otherwise manifestation will be spontaneous.

Caution: With such great resources available, hoarding is not allowed. It is as though a big bank account is not allowed, but a big salary is. The *trick* is to allow the flow and to let it move through your life ever more rapidly.

Sagittarius Part of Fortune

Sagittarius Part of Fortune describes the outcome of balancing the nodes as wisdom or enlightenment. Supply will then become a *side-effect* of the rising level of awareness. Such beings come into life as wise ones/magi and expand that capacity through the ability to expand the dimensions of their awareness. This placement is an expansion of the Scorpio placement.

Financial Affirmation: Again, with the energy flowing smoothly, there will be no need for an affirmation. This native is to allow the level of need perceived to rise. This is a matter of seeing more than personal need. It moves attention to the needs attached to our mission in life. Remember that Sagittarius is always some version of a teacher, so the willingness to expand our truths becomes the measure of our ability to attract goodness into our lives.

Caution: Inflated egos or self importance will limit the flow of good. The enlightenment given must be shared with all who seek it. Travel or publication may be a benefit if these serve the need of enlightenment. While it is best to require students to pay something for learning, it is important that teachers not tie the abundance sought to the mission. Do the work, charge reasonably, and allow this amount to be expanded to meet the needs of the mission, including all the needs and desires of the missionary. Remember, many people learn more from an example than from lessons. Be willing to accept the abundance inherent in this placement, if only for the sake of illustration.

Capricorn Part of Fortune

Capricorn Part of Fortune describes the outcome of balancing the nodes as the *rights of adulthood*, meaning the right to set our own limits and change them as we will. After the great expansion in consciousness that occurs in Sagittarius comes the responsibility for putting the Sagittarian principles into solid Capricorn form. This is the placement of the manager of the family estate. Capricorn Part of Fortune confers full dominion as a result of full maturity.

Financial Affirmation: Here the *affirmation* becomes a command or demand as we claim our right to do so. This placement makes us an agent for the owner of the *kingdom* called Earth. We speak for the owner and with the owner's authority. Our instructions come from the Creator of Life. The primary expectation is that others respect our rights, not making unreasonable demands on our time or resources.

Caution: We are expected to use this authority responsibly. We may discipline, but we abuse (anything, anyone, especially the self) only at the risk of losing everything. This is the culmination of the fusion of love and wisdom which began in Scorpio. Fear may be attached to this placement, requiring us to consciously affirm each previous level before we are willing to take the reins of power.

Aquarius Part of Fortune

Aquarius Part of Fortune describes the outcome of balancing the nodes as a reaction to inherent creativity (Leo). It also refers to the evolutionary possibilities derived from self-realization. An Aquarian magnetic field will attract inspiration from the Cosmos. Integrating all that we have understood in Sagittarius and proved in Capricorn results in a changed *form* or intent. Such a lifetime is about summarizing where we have been so that we can choose or affirm our future. We literally use our future to pull our being toward it, which is a reversal from the previous need to *push* onward. This Fortuna has no obvious connection with supply. At this level supply is assured and attention is turned in another direction.

Financial Affirmation: The simple affirmation of what we want to change or evolve becomes the magnetic vortex that will draw the necessary energy/essence and/or knowledge necessary for the change. Hopes and wishes become magnetic as the future needs determine the foundation of experience. A reversal of flow from the earlier placements occurs as the *higher* needs and desires determine their expression in the *lower* realms. What we will need in the next phase of life determines what we are doing or affirming now.

This can seem like a displacement in time, so it is extraordinarily important to refuse judgement by self or others. There is an absolute need to rely on our own inspired knowledge, and let that be the foundation of all that we do. This Part of Fortune magnetizes inspiration and inventiveness from the future establishing certain possibilities in the current consciousness. Here they layering energy. Here they attract attention and thought until they have accumulated enough force to *suddenly* emerge into manifestation.

Pisces Part of Fortune

Pisces Part of Fortune describes the outcome of balancing the nodes as unconscious. When the nodes are balanced, no further attention to creating or attracting what we want or need will be necessary. Such persons automatically attract the help and gifts that are needed to continue as the masters that they are. These mystics may seem almost to be floating above the earth, because their magnetic field is so wide as to be nearly invisible.

When the magnetic field was Aquarius, a choice was made that involved either a turning away from earth or a turning back for some previously overlooked purpose. If it was to turn away and return to Source, the next manifestation will be in Pisces. Here the native is so near to a state of pure being-ness—of full realization of godhood—as to have almost no need to magnetize anything. What is needed is already inherent in being, naturally in the hands or so close as to require very little reach. If it seems out of reach, someone will bring it, almost at the moment when it is realized as a need/desire. Thus the magnetic field may be called a *Field of Dreams*—either daydreams or night dreams, usually both—this is a *breathing* sign.

On a more mundane level the outcome of balancing the nodes will be psychic development. The only qualifier on this Part of Fortune is the definition of mastery. One may master anything from walking to driving a car to teleporting to Arcturus. With Pisces Part of Fortune the possibilities are as unlimited as the imagination.

Financial Affirmation: Anything you can imagine can be had. Imagine or envision anything and it will be yours. If you can imagine yourself having it, look around and you will find it there. Pick it up and use it.

Caution: The only real difficulty attached to this placement is a lack of trust. It is imperative that we trust our senses and believe what we can see. The only *learning* attached is the realization that anyone who can receive images can also send them. This is the synthesis of intuition and creativity.

Part of Fortune in the Houses

Part of Fortune is usually interpreted at the house level, and from that interpretation derived its name and its reputation as luck. Luck has been traditionally regarded as events that happened without apparent cause or purpose. It has been sensed that they have a Uranian flavor, and they do. Still, even Uranus may be understood and consciously used.

Very often the lucky events of life are those that the individual has long hoped for, even worked to bring about. When the manifestation occurs, it is usually dramatic, larger, or greater than was hoped or expected. They can also fall in the category of the unusual, something which mathematical minds would figure odds against. Correspondingly, the *unlucky* events are usually those we feared or worried about. In the biblical book of Job, we find Job's statement that what he feared had come upon him.

By house placement, together with aspects, Part of Fortune describes the general attitude toward luck that existed in the environment of the young child. It will describe the kind of things that are regarded as in the domain of luck, the things that are unearned and more than we deserve. It is this attitude that keeps the house of Part of Fortune in just that realm, for it may not occur to us that we can have a hand in creating our own luck.

When interpreting Part of Fortune it is important to examine the contents of the house in which it is placed to see what *makes us lucky*.

Example 1: Lucky to be____, to have _____, to learn ____, to feel ____, that I can act ____, that I function_____. (Houses 1-6)

Example 2: Lucky not to be ____, not have ____, not to feel ____, not to react ____, to be unconscious of _____. (Houses 7-12)

Several of these, if held in consciousness, have the ability to create some serious *bad luck* in our adult lives. Remember that the ego interpretation is just something you learned, not an absolute. What we learn, we can unlearn, or find a new meaning or use for.

The effects of Part of Fortune are commonly regarded as karma or dharma, good or bad effects of an earlier incarnation. This is true only in the abstract. We will choose our life circumstances based on what we think we deserve. Our own self-evaluation and/or judgments are the basis of our choices of time and place for incarnation. The Part of Fortune is then a result of how well we do or do not apply ourselves to the intent of incarnation and what that intent was. It might be regarded as the rewards we give ourselves for job performance.

Realistically, the activity or lack of it, that Part of Fortune designates is simply a side effect of activity and attitude in the environmental context. As Martin Schulman suggested, it may be more accurate to regard this point as a place where joy comes as a reward for effort. As such it must be defined in the context of the metaphysical meaning of the house structure. This begins with understanding it differently than it was taught in the beginning.

The original teaching is that each house polarity is composed of one positive[69] and one negative[70]. The social teaching is that the first seven houses belong to the child and the second seven to the adult. Metaphysical teaching includes them all as abilities, capacities, and talents—none of which are negative—that are brought into life in support or expression of the incarnational purpose.

Each house placement has three levels of expression based on the three facets of each house. Only a complete reading of the natal horoscope can produce a reasonable estimate of how Part of Fortune is currently working and how far personal consciousness will rise, lifting its meaning up into clarity and visibility. To the degree that we are not allowed to hope, wish, or dream of a better future during childhood, we will struggle to find meaning at Part of Fortune, or perhaps deny her existence in our lives. How sad that is, for always her gifts are lying just beyond the realm of visibility, awaiting that bit of attention which will energize them into manifestation.

Part of Fortune in the First House

Ego: This child is named lucky from the beginning. Usually has a well-favored name or face. Often the parents are highly visible in the community, wealthy, and able to provide a great deal. It is imperative to examine the psychological dynamics of the chart in order to decide whether the child is being loved and parented well, or just has parents that others envy. Some of the most wealthy and prominent parents neglect their children and even abuse them in atrocious ways. When this happens, the adult who survives this childhood may consider his or her survival a matter of luck or may refer to the self as unlucky.

Social: So long as the childhood attitude carries over, life will be created to mirror that childhood because bosses and other authority figures will mirror the father and mates will mirror the mother.

[69]First describes what I am or may be, second what I have or need, third how I may or do think or speak, fourth how/what I do/may feel, fifth how I should/do act, sixth is my purpose, function, use.

[70]Seventh is what I am not/should not be, eighth is what I do/can not have, ninth is disallowed, or incapacity to question, think or speak, tenth is unacceptable feelings and the response of others, eleventh unacceptable actions and the reactions of others, twelfth is useless and dysfunctional and the causes of effects in the sixth.

This can be a real blessing if/when realization comes. It will allow the individual to see the past clearly and rename it more appropriately. The truth will set us free to claim the real gifts of the first house fortune. When we know that our luck is a reward for being what we are, it will rename us.

Examples: Healthy, wealthy and/or wise, god/goddess, magi, light being.

On the positive side, if the child really was *lucky,* she or he will continue in the expectation that the original provision blessing will continue. This will allow a nice outflow from the South Node and this individual will be a blessing to others. The only difficulty from this expression at the social level is that natives may also attract envy or dependency from the seventh house as a response or reaction to being thought lucky. Affirm that the *luck* extends to relationships so that it can be experienced as an aspect of adulthood.

Spiritual: The realization of self as both blessed and a blessing is the truly spiritual meaning of this placement. Depending on how close to the Ascendant Fortuna lies, the very form of life will be defined by its magnetic field, and the native, being naturally attractive, will attract good things. If she or he is willing to share the blessing, to include others in the *circle of blessing* of which we are the center, the blessings will multiply. All who are part of this native's life will be blessed by the association. The circle will grow and grow as Part of Fortune expands through the entire chart.

Part of Fortune in the Second House

Ego: It is said that this native has luck as a personal asset. Things seem to come easily to him or her. Examine the house contents to see what it is that comes easily. This gives an attractive body, which may or may not be a gift if it attracts sexual advances at too young an age. The second contains *earned money*. For children, this is usually an abstraction. Sometimes this is learned as a need for luck. In extreme cases it may be attached to a gambling addiction.

Social: If the child has luck, the adult does not. When the childhood attitude carries over, the luck, good or bad, goes with it. Necessary transformation usually comes in the sexual arena once it is realized that the adult difficulties mirror earlier events. It will then be possible to set some limits on what is and is not acceptable, to choose our own luck, by consciously directing the magnetic field and choosing what we want to be created.

Spiritual: Our personal assets and resources are blessed, dedicated to our highest purpose. As adults, if we invest them in our highest calling, they will multiply accordingly. Such a one has a very definite purpose on earth and is given earth resources—money and movable assets enough—to purchase the freedom to develop the talents which are also inherent in this placement. It will be important to remember the parable of the talents from the Bible, for whether talent or money, it must not be hoarded if the *luck* is to be maintained.

Part of Fortune in the Third House

Ego: Lucky to be a sibling or to be able to speak/think. Usually well-favored in intelligence, at least at the logical level. Natives usually have good vision and/or hearing, and good educational opportunities. They are considered lucky to have been born with good sense. Remember that this is an ego definition so the good is qualified by the beliefs of the adults. Like the first house Part of Fortune, this one gets attention. Always the child is *heard* and named. For further definition of the terms, look to the contents of the house.

Social: If luck depends on the sibling relationship, the scattering of adult siblings could dilute the luck. If it was learning and communication skills, those very skills could turn unlucky for the adult. When the childhood attitudes carry over, the adulthood will mirror the early childhood, with some real blessings to be realized. This mind has the ability to calculate and can *figure out* anything. This will be the adult gift that must be claimed. The senses are good and must be claimed and believed, regardless of the evidence they give.

Spiritual: This is the placement of the sensory psychic. They are clairvoyant, clairaudient, clairsentient, etc. This is the origin of their *luck*. If it remains unconscious, the luck will be intermittent because of the mutable nature of the third house. If it becomes conscious, communication based on these gifts can be a primary resource. To keep the magnetic field strong, information received must be used in some fashion to bless your own life and that of your siblings—on whatever level you view siblinghood.

Part of Fortune in the Fourth House

Ego: A lucky child of a lucky mother or in a lucky home. It may imply that, in your dependency, you are lucky to be cared for and may make independence a source of *bad luck*. This placement needs careful evaluation because it makes Part of Fortune at least part of the foundation of life. The child is somehow *born lucky*, and if everything depends on luck, the life may run all over, without any boundaries, and accomplish little, in the characteristic fashion of water.

Social: When luck is with mother and child, it may completely abandon father and adult. It will be critical for this adult to realize that a *lucky start* can be the foundation for continued, growing (Cancer grows) blessing, and a magnificent demonstration in later life. Depending on how the luck was originally defined (contents of the fourth), it may be necessary to become one's own *lucky mother* and to be reborn into a new level of luck. Women may be blessed in/by their children. Usually any conscious use of the magnetic field by adults is deferred until an age when the children are or would be grown.

Spiritual: This child is blessed from birth and has many talents to grow into. She or he will encounter few real obstacles on the path to self-realization because she or he has the capacity to go under, around, or through anything which the general consciousness or his or her own belief systems put in the way. The true blessing of this placement is that the native is a channel through which blessings flow. These blessings are for personal growth and development and are only for others when/if/after a rebirth occurs. This placement shows developing Christ Consciousness, and sometimes produces a monk or nun.

Part of Fortune in the Fifth House

Ego: This may be the *lucky child* of a *lucky father* or inherited luck. Usually it refers to inherited gifts or talents. This placement can be a child prodigy or child star with all the possible range of experience that goes with it. Look carefully at parenting to see what price the child may be required to pay. If it is too high the talent may be relinquished and allowed to disappear during the socialization period of life.

Social: If the childhood attitude carries too far into adulthood, there may be an arrogant attitude that masks the lack of a real childhood foundation. This can lead to a dramatic fall from grace. Only if the luck is understood as true blessing can it continue to support the graceful direction of life established in the child. Otherwise life will react with crisis to force the native into a new role.

Spiritual: For this native, the role is the blessing. In some way the activity of childhood blesses the self, gaining much attention and *feeding*. A strong constitution is provided and natives are able to survive even the most difficult childhood or most strenuous or abused adulthood. In the end, even the rebirth, which a misuse of creativity requires, will seem to come as a lucky coincidence.

Part of Fortune in the Sixth House

Ego: Lucky to be healthy. With attention fixated in this way, the suggestion is that someone else in the childhood is not healthy. If so, the luck may bring a lot of hard work with it, and the child may not feel so lucky. It also plants the idea that health is a matter of luck and can lead to abuse or neglect of the body.

Social: If the blessing of health has become a curse of work and lost childhood, the adult may develop illness from the stress or overcompensation. Interestingly enough, sick adults can attract someone who will take care of them as they once cared for the adult in their childhood. This promotes a co-dependent relationship in which there is always one sick and one healthy participant.

Spiritual: When good health is considered a blessing, as something we are thankful for, it will continue as a perfectly functioning body and extend to a life that is both useful and fun. The placement really means that we incarnate with the knowledge of having a blessed function. We are *servants of the most high, or workers in the vineyards*. It is to be remembered that while this is a kind of yoke, Jesus said that his yoke was easy and his burden light. This placement is about exchanging the hard work of our ego beliefs for the easy function promised by our heritage as offspring of Deity. That opportunity will be presented as often and in as many forms as is necessary to bring our own innate perfection to consciousness. This is the placement of *blessing consciousness* or *blessed consciousness*. It is the fulfillment of the individuation process.

Part of Fortune in the Seventh House

Ego: Considered unlucky from birth. Luck belongs to others. They get the breaks, I have to work for all I get. The only way I can have luck is to share in someone else's good fortune. Sometimes it means that luck is not considered relevant to childhood.

Social: With awareness the adult can claim the deferred luck as soon as she or he is fully emancipated from the family of birth. Claimed, it could bless the marriage or at least the mate, and bring a share of blessing to the native. Unclaimed, it could bless the mate in ways that would trigger envy or anger in the native, leading to divorce and loss of whatever share of luck had come with the marriage. Usually it brings a sense that in order to claim our own luck we must be married. This will create more marital assets than personal ones.

Spiritual: The blessed relationship refers to the true marriage, *made in heaven*, which is the partnership between the invisible and the visible forms of spirit. It is a conscious relationship—especially a partnership—between God and Self. The awareness of this relationship leads to the realization that being the offspring of LOVE means that we inherit divine genetics. We are, therefore, magnetic, attractive, beings and can call in anything which we need or want. This is a literal expression of being *made in the image (reflection) of God.*

Part of Fortune in the Eighth House

Ego: Luck is not good—for you, for children, etc. It literally refers to an attractiveness that seemingly does the child no good, possibly does it ill. Commonly, it refers to sexual attractiveness, which is usually not an asset for a child. More literally it refers to hidden or secret attractiveness, again with questionable results for a child. As a side effect, it often leads to surgery on the sexual organs simply because the young child learned that its sexual aspects were unlucky, or no good.

Social: Any luck to be gained will usually be deferred until adulthood. This can be far into the physical adult stage because of the fused boundaries created by physical or emotional incest. The best unconscious effect of this placement is that the native is generally lucky in his or her sexual liaisons. She or he will usually be protected from disease and may profit financially.

With the effects of the eighth house Part of Fortune under judgment, it is important to remember that it is the house of rebirth. At some point the secret will out and the truth will set the native free to be born again into a new placement. Symbolically, the rebirth will fuse the second and eighth houses, allowing the native to claim the personal blessing of the second house on the structure of the adult life. Depending on the level of personal evolution, there will be a religious or spiritual rebirth.

Spiritual: The eighth house Part of Fortune attracts opportunities for a rebirth. Depending on the resistance involved, crises will intervene with regularity and/or severity. There is a pre-incarnational intent to turn this life around and head it in a new direction, so intense that it literally drives the life. This is not an easy placement, but it is intensely powerful. By investing our lives into a bonded relationship with THE FORCE, we have the power to form or reform anything.

Part of Fortune in the Ninth House

Ego: Lucky in your beliefs. Child is lucky to be born into a family that is of the "correct" religion or philosophy. A subtle or overt statement is being made that "we are on the right path, and to remain blessed, we must remain on it." This can refer to such diverse ideas as sportspersons or having something to do with the care and training of animals that can be used to work for humans. Usually it is just a heavy religious dogma that threatens bad luck if you leave it—especially the bad luck called hell. Most obviously it suggests belief without question, whether of parents or THE CHURCH.

Social: If you stay with the beliefs of your childhood, your luck/blessings will remain. If you depart, it will leave you. Since this is a Sagittarian house, the beliefs are often a composite of several or many ideas that may not be rational. To the extent that they are irrational, they will trigger rebirth in your belief system allowing an expansion of the boundaries of consciousness. The fusion with the third house will be less obvious, and sometimes less complete, than a second-eight one, but it will work well for the individual.

Spiritual: This placement literally allows the native to attract anything that she or he believes is possible. Usually the most significant growth will be in learning to stop deferring blessings to the future and call them into the present. The spiritual path is a blessed journey. The more consciously it is made the more good it will attract. The blessing is inherent in the expansion of awareness. Going farther brings greater the blessing.

Fortuna in the Tenth House

Ego: Child is lucky to have the father, authority figure, disciplinarian, or manager that she or he does. Possibly the child will be lucky to achieve adulthood and/or to have a father. Luck or blessing may be up there or out there somewhere, but not accessible until after mid-life. By reflection, Part of Fortune near the Midheaven is an unlucky birth. It may refer to the family circumstances or illegitimacy, or simply to being born in the wrong gender, place in the family, etc.

Social: Lucky to overcome the birth circumstances. A belief that success is a matter of luck. The public may in some way be lucky, perhaps because a parent was concerned about what people would say. Without consciousness, there could be a belief that all the luck got used up for survival and maturation. With consciousness there will be an awareness of many opportunities for advancement. Late in life, this one may achieve a public image as lucky or blessed.

Spiritual: Blessing from above. God's blessing on the entire life. This defines a strong attraction for the father, and a feeling of being protected in life. If the life is otherwise difficult, it will be protection in difficulty so that crises may slow progress, but never stop it. This one is being called by a higher love, magnetized toward his or her own future. Sometimes the physical father will become the guardian of the later years from the other side.

This placement refers to treasures laid up in heaven. All that is required to get them is to present a check on the account. Literally requires that prayer take the form of a demand for payment.

Part of Fortune in the Eleventh House

Ego: Being ignored can be lucky. Being adaptable or reactive can be lucky. Most commonly, luck is assigned to the realm of hopes and wishes. Luck may refer to having hopes or wishes manifest.

Certainly it will be considered an unusual or coincidental event.

Social: Friends, groups, and organizations are lucky. Action or anything that brings high visibility can be unlucky. Often luck is more a matter of whom you know than what you do. With difficult childhoods, this can make romantic liaisons or children act as deterrents to the native's luck.

The eleventh house is the house of transcendence, of overturning or overcoming the initial programming. As awareness rises, the groups that natives will be attracted to (the Uranian influence changed the direction of attraction) will be those whose goal is raising the general consciousness.

Spiritual: Blessings from the spiritual brotherhood. Here the magnetic pull from somewhere in the future is strong. This native is an angelic being, not entirely of this world. Look to the remainder of the chart for grounding to see whether the individual will be able to function well in a world which seems to be not his or her own.

Such a one truly exists and must live outside the general consciousness, transcending all the learned beliefs into which birth submerged him or her. Part of Fortune is the magnetic tie to universal beingness. Such beings are essentially impersonal or transpersonal; they are the true center of their own world and can have boundaries which extend to other constellations and beyond. Their gift and message is their ability to live at the center of an expanded space-time continuum, as an example of greater possibilities.

Part of Fortune in the Twelfth House

Ego: There is no such thing as luck. This can be learned as a life dedicated to works or one lived by faith. There seems to be no faith in the ability to work/earn blessings in the environment which surrounds this child. Still, from somewhere, from some unexplainable source, comes the faith which sustains the child and allows it to survive a childhood which is often extremely unhealthy, even unreal.

Social: Since the contents of the twelfth can be used anywhere, the adult use of this Part of Fortune is usually invested in work. Natives can, and often do, attract more work than most humans would be able to do. Still, they do it for long periods of time. If they succumb to the beliefs in the general consciousness about health, they may eventually become ill. Illness is a means of discovering that we can and do magnetize anything we need, whenever it is needed . . . even the opportunity to rest.

Spiritual: This Part of Fortune gives invisible blessing. Natives take for granted much that others might think lucky. They seem unaware of their lives as anything unusual or beyond the realms of ordinary or normal. Many of these seem entirely ungrounded, making those who observe wonder how they survive. Yet they are protected as they complete the last tasks in the last incarnation of the current cycle. Already their consciousness is more invisible than visible, more off the earth than on it. They, by their presence, point the way home, back to that point of origin from which we all emerged in the beginning.

www.ingramcontent.com/pod-product-compliance
Lightning Source LLC
Chambersburg PA
CBHW080539090426
42733CB00016B/2627